Pets

Gone

Green

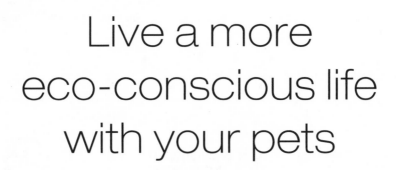

Live a more eco-conscious life with your pets

EVE ADAMSON

ORIGINAL ART BY WILLY REDDICK

Andrew DePrisco, Editorial Director
Jarelle S. Stein, Editor
Jamie Quirk, Editor
Brian Bengelsdorf, Senior Art Director
Jerome Callens, Art Director
Karen Julian, Publishing Coordinator
Melody Englund, Indexer

Printed with soy-based ink on recycled paper.

Photographs: page 8 (courtesy Eve Adamson, photo by Todd Adamson), page 159 (courtesy Eve Adamson, photo by Ben Minkler), page 160 (courtesy Willy Reddick)

Library of Congress Cataloging-in-Publication Data

Adamson, Eve.
  Pets gone green : live a more eco-conscious life with your pets / by Eve Adamson.
     p. cm.
  ISBN 978-1-59378-646-5
  1. Pets--Environmental aspects. 2. Green movement. 3. Environmental protection--Citizen participation. I. Title.

  SF413.A337 2009
  636.088'7--dc22

                        2009012639

BowTie Press®
A Division of BowTie, Inc.
3 Burroughs
Irvine, California 92618

Printed and bound in the USA
10 9 8 7 6 5 4 3 2

Dedication

To my family, in order of height: Ben, Angus, Emmett, Sally,

Jack, Grace, Snugglebunny, Ashley, Mary, Kate, Murdoch,

Elimeno, P., Emmett Jr., and Pedros 1 through 8

And to your family, no matter how many legs, tails, feathers, wings, and fins they

might have

We need another and a wiser and perhaps a more **mystical** concept of **animals.**

Remote from universal nature, and living by complicated artifice, man in civilization surveys the creature through the glass of his knowledge and sees thereby a feather magnified and the whole image in distortion. We patronize them for their incompleteness, for their tragic fate of having taken form so far below ourselves. And therein we err, and greatly err. For the animal shall not be measured by man. In a world older and more complete than ours they move finished and complete, gifted with extensions of the senses we have lost or never attained, living by voices we shall never hear. They are not brethren, they are not underlings; they are other nations, caught with ourselves in the net of life and time, fellow prisoners of the splendour and travail of the earth.

— Henry Beston,
writer and naturalist

CONTENTS

Preface

I come from a long line of women who have always been ridiculously mushy at the very thought of a warm fuzzy animal. My grandmother, my mother, my sisters, and I are all confirmed animal lovers, pet parents, and supporters of animal welfare causes. I've always been interested in environmental causes, too.

However, for most of my life I viewed mother nature as more of a real mother than anything else—a force that would take care of, nurture, and keep me and all of the other people and all the animals safe and sound.

Then I heard about the polar bears. The news that melting ice caps had reduced their habitats so much that many of these bears were drowning deeply upset me. The pictures showing polar bears stranded on tiny floating icebergs or, worse, swimming through warming waters with no iceberg anywhere in sight, touched me in a way that no theoretical knowledge about global warming ever had. Suddenly, I felt moved to do something about the problem of global warming.

Because of my concern about the environment, I had already changed a lot of my bad habits. My family generates just 25 percent of the trash we used to generate, and we are aces at curbside recycling. We buy a lot less, and we buy local products whenever we can. We walk and bike more, and we try to reduce our carbon footprint in as many other ways as possible: gradually replacing our lightbulbs with the longer-lasting kind, reusing items more, and getting most of our groceries at the

farmer's market. However, after hearing about the polar bears, I was determined to go even greener.

I spent a few emotional days fretting about how to do something important that would make a difference. Then one morning, while watching one of my two dogs chew on a brightly colored dog toy and the other one scratch furiously at his ear, I had an epiphany. My "green efforts" might not directly save a polar bear from its tragic fate, but I have animals right here in my own house, in my own family, that are affected by an increasingly toxic environment. I asked myself what I could do to save *them*.

I wrote this book for two reasons. Number one, I want to show people who have made animals a part of their families how they can live greener and make a positive impact on the earth as well as on their immediate environments. What can you do to save your animals *and* the polar bears—and maybe even the human life this planet has sustained so far? This book has some answers.

Number two, I want to plant the seed of an idea in my readers' heads: What if the best, easiest, and most permanent way to change the way we live on this planet is to think less like humans and more like the animals we love and admire?

Acknowledgments

Thanks to my kids, Angus and Emmett, for making a safe, clean, and evolved future seem a little more important. Thanks to Ben, for keeping said kids out of the office when I was working on this book and for organizing and energizing our family's recycling efforts. Thanks to the animals that share our home: Sally, Jack, Grace, Snugglebunny, and the many fishes. Each of you, in your own way, adds joy and life to our family. Thanks to my mom, for being so soft hearted, and to my dad, for being so practical. I like to think I inherited an equal measure of both qualities. Thanks to my editors at *Pet Product News International*, especially Carol Boker, Lisa King, and Anne Sedjo, for giving me the "Holistic Marketplace" column for so many years. Writing this column has given me the opportunity to meet a whole community of ethical and environmentally concerned pet product manufacturers and retailers. Thanks to *Dog Fancy* magazine, especially Susan Chaney and Annamaria Barajas, for constant support and encouragement throughout my freelance career. Thanks to my editors at BowTie Press, especially Andrew DePrisco, who first called me with the idea to write this book. It's been a lively dialogue! Thanks to my fellow Dog Writers Association of America members, for their checks and balances regarding the sometimes-volatile issues surrounding pet adoption, spay/neuter laws, and the ongoing "animal rights versus animal welfare" debate. Thanks to Caroline Coile, my dog-world anchor. Finally, thanks to all the animals. Wherever you dash, saunter, gallop, waddle, soar, crawl, creep, sleep, hop, or swim over the surface of our mother the earth, this book is for you.

Introduction

As a freelance writer, a little more than half of my income is generated from writing about animals. I write mostly about dogs but also about cats, birds, fish, garden ponds, and the pet product market. I've been doing this for more than a decade, and I have seen many trends come and go. Right now, "green" is in, so naturally I've had a lot of assignments related to eco-friendly, environmentally conscious, and green living as it relates to animals. And I started to learn some things.

After Al Gore came out with his movie, *An Inconvenient Truth, green* became a buzz-word in the industry. That movie isn't about companion animals, but it is about the earth, and it made people think about the impact of their choices. Pet product manufacturers noticed a shift in buying patterns, as more customers requested information about the eco-friendliness of products.

Then we experienced a massive pet food recall in spring 2007, after scores of cat and dog foods manufactured in China were found to contain poisonous melamine, a chemical used to make plastics. Pets were dying from organ failure because of the adulterated foods *we were feeding them.* Pet owners all over the country felt guilty, angry, and grief stricken. Natural and organic pet food sales skyrocketed, and many small holistically oriented pet store owners couldn't keep enough natural and organic foods on their shelves. Pet

food companies' phones were ringing off the hook with people demanding to know whether the companies' foods were safe and where the ingredients for those products came from. Some people even switched to making their own pet food.

The pet food market hasn't been the same since; even in a slower economy, retailers tell me the natural foods are still in great demand. Pets are part of the family, so people don't skimp on what could affect their health. People will cut back in other areas rather than reduce the quality of the lives of their companion animals.

I wrote a lot about food in the months after the recall, and I'm still writing about it. But there are more issues than food to be concerned about. Several holistic veterinarians have informed me that dogs are getting cancers of all kinds at an unprecedented rate. Although some veterinarians claim that we are just seeing the diseases

of aging that naturally occur because dogs are living longer, others vehemently disagree. They say that cancer should not be this common in dogs and that even young dogs are falling victim.

Some veterinarians who see a great deal of cancer in their practices believe there is a correlation between environment and this condition. Many holistically minded vets tell me they suspect that cancer is, at least in part, a result of ingesting the chemicals in commercially processed pet food and exposure to other sources of chemicals in our environments.

Mind you, these are not proven links. However, because pets spend a lot of time on our carpets and furniture, they come into much closer contact with any residue from the cleaning chemicals we use, not to mention pesticides and other pollutants that we track in from the outside world on our shoes.

In sensitive pets, this chemical exposure might have serious health consequences. Although many dogs and cats do not get cancer, many do have serious skin rashes, itching, hot spots, and allergies. Could these be the result of a toxic environment: a polluted planet and a chemically laced home? When I wrote an article recently about grooming products, I learned how many harsh chemicals they can contain. Are we poisoning our animals every time that we give them baths?

And what about human beings? Are processed food and environmental toxins affecting us and our children as well? As a mother, this notion strikes me to the heart, especially when it seems that greater numbers of people are getting cancer at younger ages. If our cavalier attitude toward the earth has resulted in a situation that has put us all—our families, including our animal companions, as well as the animals out there in the natural world—in danger, if we are poisoning ourselves with the products we use in our homes and on our own bodies, the air we breathe, the water we drink, the food we eat, then shouldn't we be doing something about it? My job, after all, is to protect the children and animals in my own home, a microcosm of our planet. It's all enough to give us nurturing types a severe panic attack.

But this book isn't about panicking. It's about finding a way to improve our current situation by living greener. I believe the way to do this, and to live more simply, is closer than you might think. I believe that it is sitting beside you, gazing at you with adoring eyes.

Animals don't experience the world in the same way people do. They smell more of it, hear more of it, and feel more of it, from whiskers to tail. Even domesticated animals understand better than we do how to move through the world and read the natural signs, and they certainly don't treat the world the way we do. Any trash thrown into landfills on behalf of animals is certainly our doing, not theirs.

If you live with and care about an animal, you are in direct contact with the natural world in a way that other people, inside their climate-controlled houses and cars, may never experience. You have a little piece of nature, right there in your own home, right there in your lap. You see echoes of the wolf or the tiger as well as a mirror into your own soul. Our companion animals help us see how all of life is bound together. We share an ecosystem, breathing the same air, drinking the same water, eating the same food. We share many of the same daily experiences, and we may even share some far-distant relatives.

Even domesticated animals understand better than we do how to move through the world and read the natural signs, and they certainly don't treat it the way we do.

If you want to get spiritual about it, you could say we share the same energy, flowing in and out and around all of us. No doubt, we are all tied together, you, your animals, me, my animals, and the earth itself. Although some people take their pets for granted, others see life with a companion animal as a privilege and an inroad to understanding the world in all its variety and mystery. Animals have lessons to teach us about how to live more lightly on the earth. Their needs are usually simple—and maybe ours are, too. Maybe we just complicate things with our overevolved brains. What if the animals have the right idea, and we are the ones going in the wrong direction? If you really do care about the earth and preserving the natural world that supports you and your animals, the real question becomes: What are you going to do about it?

I've read a lot of books about how to go green, raise your eco-consciousness, and reduce your carbon footprint, and after a while, they all start to sound the same. They start with all the statistics that prove the world has a problem, then they launch into lists about how the average Joe or Jane can make a difference: turn off the water when you brush your teeth, switch out your lightbulbs to more energy-efficient types, and recycle your trash.

This book is different. I'm going to assume that you believe something needs to be done to stop our cavalier treatment of our home planet and that you are already doing some basic things to reduce your carbon footprint, such as recycling, trying to drive less, trying to use less. If you are eating organic food, adjusting your thermostat, recycling your trash, and taking your canvas bag to the grocery store, then you *are already making a difference*. Every little thing you do to make less of a harmful impact on the planet is a good thing.

But in this book, I would like to challenge you to start thinking beyond the box that I will label "humanness." When we live with, love, and respect our companion animals, we have an amazing opportunity to start looking beyond our own narrow needs into another, broader, bigger universe that honors all life. What would happen if we tweaked our lives to be a little more in tune with the animals that share them? This book is about how to do that, because changing your mind is the first step toward changing the world. When you change the way in which you think, then your actions change naturally, and that's how you can finally stick to an earth-friendlier existence.

This book is about how to live green with your animals, for your animals, and by taking a cue from your animals.

Animals know some things we've forgotten, and remembering them can change our lives, and the planet, for the better. In this book, I'll make some suggestions and offer guidance based on what I've learned about companion animals over the twelve-plus years I've been writing about them, but then I hope you and your animals will forge your own kinder, gentler, and more earth-respectful path.

As I encourage you to tap into your animal companion's natural wisdom, I also want to encourage you to start looking beyond the surface level of what you do, so that you begin to see how it all works together, how we are all connected. When you start thinking more *holistically*—recognizing how every part influences the whole—then the differences you make as you change your habits will start to have real power. That's when you can take the next step—acting on your beliefs. If you take nothing else away from this book, I hope you will take this: if you figure out what you believe, find out whether it is true, and then *do* what you think is right, you can change the world. This is the ultimate, underlying message of *Pets Gone Green.* That is how we can take this whole "life" thing to the next level.

To live a greener life, you don't have to agree with every point raised in this book or take every suggestion. You don't have to buy organic or quit eating meat or forget your dreams of a purebred dog companion. I am not trying to criticize or to judge anyone. In order to live a greener life, however, you do need to think beyond our limited human nature. It is your journey, your life, and in the end your reckoning.

Yet, at the same time, you are never alone. Each one of us is on the same journey, and when we work together, we can make change happen. If you care about the world that gives you and your family food, trees, fresh air, flowers, fields, mountains, oceans, lakes, rivers, and yes, animal friends, then I hope that this book will mean something to you.

May we and generations of our descendants live together in harmony on this planet for many thousands of years to come.

Chapter 1

Recycled
Companions

The Ultimate

Earth-Friendly

Act

The first time I saw Rally Sally, I was browsing through the animal shelter, *just to see*. I didn't think I'd find a dog who spoke to me. I meandered down the aisles looking at the animals, and then I caught sight of her: a small, skinny, white and brown smooth-coated terrier mix who fixed me with a hypnotic stare.

I stared back, and it was as if she were speaking to me, mind to mind: *You will take me home*. So I did, and I found myself with the most intelligent, resourceful, clever, and devoted animal friend I have ever had. Sally is my heart dog; I cannot imagine life without her.

Where did your dog or cat or bird or hamster come from? And where will you find your next animal companion? How you decide to bring an animal into your life is one of the most important pet-related decisions that you can make, one that has serious environmental repercussions. Pet store? Breeder? Internet? Animal shelter? Rescue group? What is the eco-conscious—and, by association, the most humane—choice?

Green Words

It is an important and popular fact that things are not always what they seem. For instance, on the planet Earth, man had always assumed that he was more intelligent than dolphins because he had achieved so much—the wheel, New York, wars and so on—whilst all the dolphins had ever done was muck about in the water having a good time. But conversely, the dolphins had always believed that they were far more intelligent than man—for precisely the same reasons.

—Douglas Adams,
author, *The Hitchhiker's Guide to the Galaxy*

When their pets become inconvenient, some people throw them away, like trash, dumping them at animal shelters. Other people reluctantly relinquish their animals because changed circumstances—illness, divorce, death—have made it difficult or impossible to keep them. Whatever the reason an animal ends up in a shelter or with a rescue group, the fact is that animal has been discarded. When you decide to adopt one of these pets rather than buy one "new," you are, in a real sense, recycling.

There are many other benefits to adopting an animal from a shelter or rescue group. These organizations often address medical problems and fund training programs for their adoptable animals to minimize future behavioral issues. The animals may already be used to living in a home with people, and they are often housetrained and well socialized. The older animals are through with the many challenges of puppyhood or kittenhood, such as house-training accidents, destructive chewing, and high energy.

Animal shelters and rescue groups around the country have millions of animals waiting for homes. A huge percentage of those animals will be euthanized every year because nobody adopted them.

So why buy new when you can recycle?

Animal Shelters

Most communities have animal shelters or animal control facilities. The Humane Society of the United States (HSUS) estimates that there are between 4,000 and 6,000 animal shelters in the United States, processing 6 to 8 million cats and dogs every year, so you probably have one near you. These facilities go by many names. Some call themselves SPCAs (societies for the prevention of cruelty to animals) or humane societies. Others are simply called animal shelters. Some are connected with city or county animal control programs, and others are privately run.

Many struggle for funds and staff. Others (although not many) have a lot of funding. Some have the resources to evaluate incoming animals carefully, while others barely have the resources to bring the animals in at all. Some shelters euthanize animals that aren't adopted in a timely manner. Others, sometimes called no-kill shelters, adopt out or keep and care for all the animals they take in so they won't have to euthanize any pets.

Before you decide where to adopt an animal, do some research and find out what kind of animal sheltering options exist

Green Facts

According to the National Council on Pet Population Study and Policy, only one of the top ten reasons for relinquishing a dog to an animal shelter in the United States has anything to do with behavior issues (#9). Those reasons are:

1. Moving
2. Landlord issues
3. Cost of pet maintenance
4. No time for the pet
5. Inadequate facilities
6. Too many pets in the home
7. Pet illness
8. Personal problems
9. Biting
10. No homes for littermates

Only two of the top ten reasons for relinquishing a cat to an animal shelter in the United States have to do with behavior (#7 and #10). Those reasons are:

1. Too many cats in the house
2. Allergies
3. Moving
4. Cost of pet maintenance
5. Landlord issues
6. No homes for littermates
7. House soiling
8. Personal problems
9. Inadequate facilities
10. Doesn't get along with other pets

Green Stats

There are approximately 74.8 million owned dogs and 88.3 million owned cats in the United States, according to the American Pet Products Manufacturers Association (APPMA) 2007–2008 National Pet Owners Survey.

in your community. If you live in a large town or city, you will probably have many options. Check the searchable shelter database of the American Society for the Prevention of Cruelty to Animals (ASPCA) at www.aspca.org. (Click on "Adoption," then click on "Search Our Shelter Database.") It comprises nearly 5,000 community SPCAs, humane societies, and animal-control facilities. Or check the Petfinder Web site at www.petfinder.org.

Even if you want a purebred pet, look at the animal shelter first. HSUS estimates that 25 percent of dogs in shelters are purebreds. Additionally, many shelters work with purebred rescue groups, so shelter workers may be able to direct you to relevant resources (see the next section on rescue groups).

The worst thing you can do when looking for an animal companion is to rush into your decision. After all, when you make a significant purchase, such as a car, a home, or even a smart phone, you spend time considering which one is right for you. Otherwise, you might find, once you get it home, that it wasn't the right choice. Doesn't an animal deserve even more careful consideration? Impulse buying an animal is much more likely to result in a bad match and problems later—ones that often result in the return of a pet to the shelter.

Some people are hesitant to adopt an animal that someone else has

REDUCE YOUR Carbon Pawprint

Keep your own animals and others out of the animal shelter. Here's how:

Commit to your animals. If you bring a companion animal into your home and family, commit to a permanent situation. After all, if your kids cause trouble, you help them; you don't give them away.

License your animals, and be sure they always wear identification tags, even indoors. If these animals ever end up lost and make it to the shelter, you'll have a much better chance of reclaiming them. Having the shelter or a veterinarian implant an identifying microchip in your animal can also help identify your animal if its tags are lost or taken off.

Spay or neuter your animals to avoid creating more unwanted animals (see chapter 3 for more on this issue). Encourage others to spay/neuter. Tell others whether the local shelters or certain vet clinics offer low-cost spay/neuter options.

Green Shelters

given up because they fear the animal has something wrong with it. Sometimes, this is true. Like children in foster homes, some animals develop behavior problems as a result of neglect and/or abandonment. However, many of them are amazing, loyal, sweet, devoted animals that already know how to live with humans (such as my Rally Sally). Others need just a little bit of time and extra patience.

The best way to avoid problems is to do your research and ask questions. Before you adopt an animal from a shelter, get as much of the story as you can. Don't be shy. Ask the shelter or rescue group:

- How do you screen the animals?
- What do you know about this animal's history?
- Do you know whether this animal gets along with other pets?
- Do you know whether this animal gets along with children?
- Does this animal have any health issues I should know about?
- Does this animal have any behavioral issues?

Many shelters do their part by carefully screening you to be sure you have the time, resources, and knowledge to take care of a companion animal—and that pets are allowed where you live. Some shelters also require you to bring everyone in your

Adopting from a shelter is an eco-conscious act, but adopting from a green shelter doubles the power of the green. The Leadership in Energy and Environmental Design (LEED) Green Building Rating System certifies buildings that are designed, constructed, and operated according to environmentally responsible and healthful standards. The Tompkins County SPCA in Ithaca, New York (www.spcaonline.com/new_green.htm), and the Winnipeg Humane Society in Canada (www.winnipeghumanesociety.ca/) have LEED-certified buildings. Other green shelters include the Potter League for Animals, in Middletown, Rhode Island; the Humane Society Silicon Valley, in California; the Bow Valley SPCA, in Alberta, Canada; Dallas Animal Services, in Texas; City of Sacramento Animal Care Services, in California; the Humane Society of Huron Valley, in Michigan; the Washington Animal Rescue League, in the District of Columbia; and Watermelon Mountain Ranch Animal Center, in Rio Rancho, New Mexico, just outside of Albuquerque.

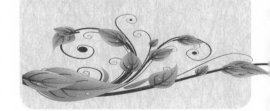

household in to make sure that all of them are on board with the adoption and that everyone gets along with the potential pet. Even if a shelter doesn't have this requirement, it's a good idea for you to take family members with you for this purpose.

Sometimes, shelters won't allow people to adopt if they have very young children, can't provide written documentation from a landlord stating that pets are allowed, or don't have what the shelter deems to be proper facilities to house the animal. Some shelters have policies prohibiting students from adopting a pet, because they have seen too many pets abandoned at the end of a semester or school year. Rejection by an animal shelter drives some people to pet stores, but consider this: if the shelter staffers say you shouldn't have a pet at the present time, maybe they are right.

Rescue Groups and Purebreds

Although I live with a couple of lovable mutts, I, like many other people, appreciate the history and tradition behind the purebred dog. In fact, I often write about purebred animals. People who want a purebred dog or cat are often drawn to specific qualities and know they can find them most reliably in certain breeds. If you really want a purebred, you can still make an eco-conscious and compassionate choice by going to a purebred rescue group.

The Evolution of Breeds

Although the climate, the influence of indigenous dogs in a particular area, and other aspects of natural selection also played a part, humans actually "created" most breeds through selective breeding, including sled dogs, guard dogs, herding dogs, terriers, hound dogs, gun dogs, war dogs, service dogs, and toy dogs. Even before our intercession, dogs in different regions had evolved to look and behave differently from one another. Hardy arctic dogs, for instance, grew thicker coats than desert dogs, which, in addition to having thinner coats, were rangier and more heat tolerant than their cold-weather brethren.

But humans nudged along desirable behaviors in dogs by rewarding, and therefore ensuring, the survival and more prolific procreation of dogs that acted in ways beneficial to humans. We also managed to shape dogs physically by choosing the looks we preferred and helping them thrive through breeding, making dogs bigger or smaller, with different kinds and colors of coats, short or long noses, short or long ears, tight or loose skin, big or small eyes, small or large paws, strong or gentle jaws, and cautious or totally trusting temperaments.

Whether you think we should have gotten involved in breed creation or not, the fact is that we're still doing it. For example, witness the new "designer dog" craze, with its Labradoodles, Puggles, and other mixes popping up in pet stores all the time. Purebreds exist and have a long shared history with humans. To some people, that is worth preserving.

Domesticated cats evolved in much the same way. A mutual fascination developed, and we took cats into our homes. Then we began to see what we could do with them. In the purebred cat world, a new mutation pops up, and somebody loves the cat and

Green Facts

The term **purebred** means an animal, such as a dog, cat, or horse, with certain established traits, cultivated through selective breeding, reliably produces more dogs or cats or horses with those same traits when bred with an animal of the same breed. The term **pedigreed** means an animal has a record of ancestors proving it is a purebred and comes from ancestors of the same breed. A pedigreed animal is always a purebred, but a purebred animal might not be pedigreed if there are no records to prove it is a purebred. But the words are often used interchangeably.

its look so much that she vows to turn it into a new breed. The American Curl, the LaPerm, the Scottish Fold, and the Ocicat are a few examples, all transformed into officially recognized purebreds during the second half of the twentieth century.

Some people think that purebred animals have more serious health problems than mixed breeds do. Others (including many veterinarians) dispute this, claiming that all dogs and cats can have health issues, but that with purebreds, we are better able to predict what those issues might be. Many purebreds are healthy, vigorous animals that can still do the job they were

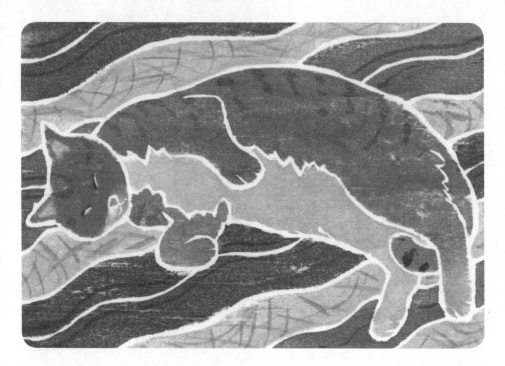

originally bred to do, whether that is hauling in a boat or a drowning swimmer (just try to stop the Newfoundland from pulling your kids out of the pool), rounding up a wayward flock of sheep (Border Collies have what it takes), keeping the rats out of the barn (talk to the Fox Terrier or the Maine Coon), or sitting in your lap listening to all your problems (the Shih Tzu is a pro, and so is the Persian).

The Rescue Groups

If you have your heart set on a purebred cat or dog or a more unusual animal such as a parrot, ferret, or goat, look to rescue groups. These privately run and often exclusively volunteer-fueled organizations range from the very informal (someone's taking in cats until good homes can be found for them) to the very rigorous (large highly organized purebred rescue groups with national transportation networks to deliver rescued dogs to the right foster homes and then to

Green Facts

According to the Save the Tiger Fund, a program of the National Fish and Wildlife Foundation, there are only about 5,000 to 7,400 wild tigers left in the world—just 7 percent of the wild tiger population of a century ago. By contrast, there are about 88.3 million domestic cats in the United States alone, according to the APPMA 2007–2008 National Pet Owners Survey.

good permanent homes). Rescue groups typically specialize in certain breeds (such as Golden Retrievers, Border Collies, or Siamese cats) or types of animals (such as birds, small animals, or farm animals). Some also specialize in senior pets or animals with special needs.

Like the best animal shelters, rescue groups are fairly picky about whom they will allow to adopt a pet. The animals they take in have already been abandoned once, and these folks don't want to see it happen again. Many groups require extensive adoption applications, multiple home visits, and a lot of personal information. Just remember, what seems like an intrusion into your privacy is all done with the best intentions and in the animal's best interest.

Many national, regional, and local purebred dog and cat clubs also run or sponsor related rescue groups devoted to that club's breed of choice. Others aren't affiliated with anyone. The great thing about rescue groups is that there are so many. The bad thing is that they aren't all equal in quality or in their ability to screen and determine the adoptability of animals. Some, unfortunately, are actually puppy mills in disguise, people collecting animals to resell, or even animal hoarders who have a psychological addiction to collecting animals.

Look into any rescue group you work with carefully to ensure the group is what it claims to be. Ask to talk to previous adopters, and call them to find out about their experience with the rescue group. Ask the rescue group a lot of questions about how it screens for health and behavior as well as what it requires from adopters.

Find out everything you can about an animal's past, then be prepared, no matter how much information you are given, for some surprises. Animals that have been passed around for a while tend to have some behavior problems, even though these problems can almost always be fixed with the right training.

If a purebred appeals to you, you can probably find a purebred rescue group specializing in the animal you seek. Consult the following resources:

Your local animal shelter may work directly with purebred and other specific kinds of rescue groups. The staff may even send any purebred

REDUCE YOUR Carbon Pawprint

If you love the idea of helping rescued animals but can't commit long term to an adoption, consider volunteering at an animal shelter or providing a foster home for rescued pets while they wait for permanent homes. You will be facilitating animal adoptions and filling a great need. You'll also be making a positive impact on how our society treats our animal friends and, by extension, the earth.

animals they get to rescue groups, so ask there first.

🐾 Your veterinarian might know of good local rescue groups, and may also be able to steer you away from any who aren't acting in the best interest of animal health.

🐾 Your local dog or cat club may know who is rescuing animals in your area.

🐾 Local pet stores that sell pet supplies—but not animals—may know of good groups. Some work directly with these groups to facilitate adoption.

In addition, there are hundreds of rescue organizations on the Internet. Some serve limited areas, while others network many rescue groups and volunteers together. A few good ones are listed below.

Petfinder, www.petfinder.com: This Web site has access to a massive database that allows you to search by the kind of animal, breed, age, size, gender, and location. Find dogs, cats, birds, horses, pigs, rabbits, small animals, and other barnyard animals here. Check back often. Petfinder is a great resource for the would-be adopter.

American Kennel Club (AKC), www.akc .org: To find purebred dog rescue groups affiliated with national breed clubs, search the AKC Web site. Click on "Breeds" at the top left, then click on "Breed Rescue" on the left.

Senior Dogs Project, www.srdogs.com: This group specializes in finding homes for adopted senior dogs. Search by state; Canada is included.

Alley Cat Rescue National Cat Protection Association, www.saveacat.org: This group works to protect cats locally through rescue and adoption, and nationally through a network of cat action teams.

Purebred Cat Breed Rescue, www .purebredcatbreedrescue.org: To find purebred cat rescue groups, search this Web site.

Avian Welfare Coalition (AWC), www .birdadoption.org; and Feathered Friends Forever, www.featheredfriendsforever.org: The AWC Web site has a list of bird rescue, adoption, and sanctuary groups by state, plus lots of information on why it is better to adopt a rescued bird rather than buy a new one. Another cool place is Feathered Friends Forever, a licensed animal shelter in Georgia just for birds.

REDUCE YOUR Carbon Pawprint

If you are considering adopting a pet, consider a senior. Many people relinquish their senior pets to shelters and rescue groups when the animals develop health issues or need extra attention, and suddenly the home the animal has known all its life is gone. You may not have a senior pet for as long as you would have a younger adopted animal, but senior dogs and cats make wonderful, calm, gentle pets that just need someone to love and care for them in their golden years. Most people who adopt senior pets are very glad they did it.

nutrition and how to start socializing and even house-training the puppy before it leaves the whelping box and its mother and littermates. This environment can only be provided by a smaller-scale, responsible hobby breeder.

Profit is never the bottom line with a good breeder, as it has to be with commercial sources. To properly evaluate and choose the best breeding pairs, to hand raise and socialize the animals from birth, to give them enough time with their parents and siblings, and to give each one enough exercise and veterinary attention from birth to the day of sale is just too expensive.

Responsible Breeders

In the greenest of all possible worlds, everyone would adopt new four-legged family members from animal shelters and rescues. Recycling is our call to arms— arms that hug and welcome unwanted pets. Some dog owners, however, may want a new puppy—and who can blame them? Puppies are the *cutest.* If you are one of these puppy-love-seeking individual, and you can't find a suitable youngster at the shelter, then be sure to look for a puppy raised in an ideal atmosphere. You want one specifically and carefully bred to minimize genetic and other health problems and handled every day in a calm, caring environment by a loving human who understands and has knowledge of the puppy's needs. These include the right

GREEN GUIDE

🔥 To find a good hobby breeder who has signed a code of ethics promising to breed in the best interest of the animal, visit www.akc.org, the Web site of the American Kennel Club—the country's oldest and largest purebred dog registry—and click on "Breeds" at top. Then click on "Breeder Referral," on the left. Better yet, click on "Breed Rescue."

🔥 To find purebred cats, check out the Cat Fanciers' Association at www.cfainc.org (click on "Breeder Referral" on the left) or the International Cat Association at www.tica.org (click on "Find a Breeder" on the left).

🔥 Better yet, check out Purebred Cat Breed Rescue: www.purebredcatbreedrescue.org.

> *We can judge the heart of a man by his treatment of animals.*
> —Immanuel Kant,
> philosopher

Small, ethical hobby breeders pour their personal resources into doing all those things because they are so passionate about their breeds. They practice dog breeding in the animal's best interest, and financial consideration is not their primary motivation. In fact, many never make a penny breeding animals, yet they have made great strides in improving the health and temperament of the breed they love. As with any hobbyist, their hobby is their *passion*, not their profession. The hobby breeder's quest is to produce a perfectly healthy, beautiful, and functional animal, and doing that means providing the best possible environment and care, both before and after birth.

The problem is that most people don't realize the difference between hobby breeders and for-profit breeders, and dogs from for-profit breeders are easier to find (making them more subject to impulse buying). The demand for purebred puppies and "designer dogs" (expensive mixed breeds, such as Labradoodles and Puggles) is high so profit-driven commercial breeders stay in business. But that doesn't mean you have to help keep them there. Ask questions and find out the size of the breeding operation (smaller is better, raising multiple breeds is a red flag), the person's motivation for breeding, whether the breeder conducts health tests or socializes the animals, and where the animals are raised (in the house or in kennels?). Always visit so you can see the other dogs and assess how they look and act.

Remember, everything you do affects everything else. We are all connected, and our actions speak loudly to the world around us. Buying a dog from a disreputable source is like voting with your dollars to support practices that disrespect the welfare of animals and use animals as a commodity. By choosing a pet from a small hobby breeder or a shelter, you might influence others to do the same. This is how you begin to change the world.

Green Facts

According to the American Humane Association, more American households have pets than have children, and we spend more money on pet food than on baby food.

Exotic Animals

Because exotic animals, such as large birds, giant snakes, and monkeys, are not domesticated, they are much more difficult to keep as pets than most people realize. Large parrots, for instance, are sweet and affectionate until they become

THE WORD *Pet*

Some people have a problem with the word *pet*. To them it sounds like a derogatory term, one implying subjugation of one species to another or suggesting that animal companions exist only for the enjoyment and amusement of humans. I disagree. While I do not believe that we should consider ourselves masters over animals, that the purpose of the animal kingdom is to serve humankind, or that my dogs are "owned" by me, I do consider myself their guardian, parent, and protector. I am responsible for them. I see animals as fellow sentient beings, some of whom have evolved to form a mutually beneficial relationship with humans. That being said, I do use the word *pet* throughout this book (and even in the lighthearted title) when it seems unwieldy to use another term. To me, *pet* is a synonym for animal companion, and I use it with the deepest gratitude for the relationship I have with the animals in my life (many of which spend much of their day coercing me to pet them). I call my children "kids" and "kiddos" (and a lot of other things, depending on my mood and their behavior at the moment), and I have no less respect for them because of those nicknames. I use the word *pet* in that same spirit of love and endearment.

sexually mature. Then they can become aggressive, loud, and extremely difficult for the average pet owner to manage. They aren't being "bad"; they are acting like they are supposed to act—in the wild. In many cases, this is the stage at which the parrot gets sent back to the pet store, the animal shelter, or the bird rescue group. As a result, thousands of birds are left without loving homes and the skills to survive on their own.

Smaller birds like parakeets and cockatiels can be affectionate and interactive pets, but they are incredibly social and need a lot of attention. Our very tame cockatiel, Grace, lives in my son's room (or wherever people are—she's good at following us around), and the door to her cage is never closed; but that isn't realistic for a lot of people. Think about how birds live in the wild, and consider how closely you can safely replicate that experience in your own home.

As for reptiles, snakes may not seem to mind sitting on a heating pad in a glass tank for years, but who knows? Besides, snakes often escape and when they are very large, that can put local wildlife at risk. Iguanas and many other reptiles are actually very active in nature, with a natural diet difficult to replicate. They aren't cuddly, and they aren't that interested in bonding with you, but they still have specific needs you have to meet if you decide to take them into your home. Is that really the kind of animal companion you want?

Many other exotics, such as monkeys and big cats (cougars and tigers, for example), are no longer legal to own, or owning them requires permits and special training because they have caused so many problems in the past when people tried to live with them.

If you are one of the rare people with the interest, knowledge, and resources to care for an exotic pet properly, please consider making the eco-conscious choice when you look for one. Exotics are profitable to sell, and some of these animals are caught in the wild and exported to the United States. Others are bred in captivity and then sold. In the case of birds, many of these are sold in "parrot mill" breeding

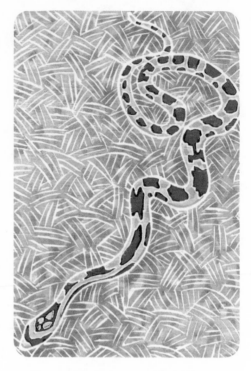

establishments similar to puppy mills.

Rather than voting with your dollars to support the practice of producing animals for profit or, even worse, taking them out of their natural environment, consider adopting a recycled exotic. There are now many more exotic animals out there than good homes for them, so if you want to make the eco-conscious choice and you really want to provide a safe refuge for an exotic animal, look to rescue. There are many bird as well as a few reptile rescue groups and lots of rabbit, ferret, and small animal rescue groups. Remember: Why buy new when you can recycle?

Green Facts

According to Interpol's Wildlife Working Group, illegal taking, trafficking, and trading of wild animals and plants is a serious problem, bringing traffickers billions of dollars in illegal profits every year. Environmental crimes, from the illegal capture and sale of tiny turtles or colorful parrots to the poaching of a giant rhinoceros or the harvesting of elephant tusks, threaten our planet's biodiversity, ecosystem, and economy, as well as human health and safety.

Green Words

Reflecting Eco-Consciousness

We share the earth with animals, and some of those animals exist in their current incarnation because of us. We created the concept of the "pet." We've filled our world with these pets, many of whom can't live or function without human intervention. And every single day in the United States, animal shelters kill dogs and cats simply because the animals have nowhere to go and we don't have anywhere to put them. Some have serious health or temperament problems. Others would have made wonderful pets if only someone had found them in time.

There is a direct correlation to our relationship with the earth here. Are we taking responsibility for what we've done to companion animals and the effects that has on our environment? We throw away trash every day; we pour pollution into our water and air; and we keep buying, buying, buying—including animals—cluttering our homes and lives with stuff we don't need. Maybe, as a society, our lack of respect for the earth and our lack of respect for companion animals are related. Could heightening our respect for one increase our awareness of and sensitivity toward the other? Of course it could. When we become more aware of what we consume and why, we start to see patterns of waste and carelessness, and that has a ripple effect that can benefit all life.

If we become hardened to the suffering of others—people or animals—then we have lost our reverence for life. Despite our many misdeeds as a society, our companion animals *love us.* When we honor that bond, we honor the natural world—and we honor ourselves. You can be totally selfish about it, if you want to be: caring about what happens to animals translates into caring about what happens to people, and when we care about what happens to one another, the world simply becomes a better place in which to live.

Chapter 2

Green
Food

The Ripple

Effect

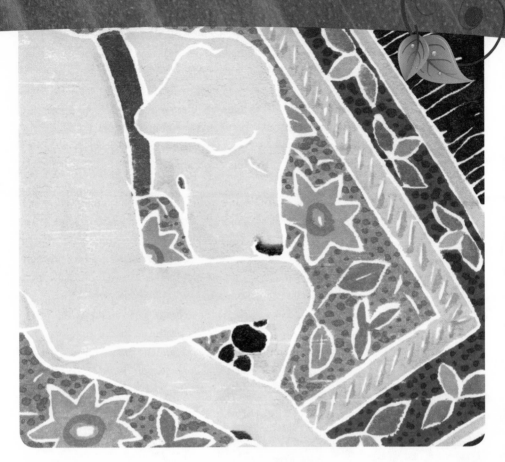

ome animals will eat just about anything. Some, such as my dogs, Jack and Sally, are fairly picky. However, our animal companions don't normally go out hunting, as they would if they were still wild dogs, and most of them don't scavenge anymore, as their feral dog ancestors did. We choose what they eat, and we influence their

environments in no greater way than via food. What you eat, and what you feed your family, including your companion animals, matters not only to their health and well-being but also to those of the planet, which provides that sustenance.

Figuring out what to feed your companion animals that will be good for them and good for the planet can be tricky, raising a lot of questions. For instance, is commercial dog food OK, or are all commercial foods suspect? Should you buy organic food? Free-range? Grain free? Vegetarian? Frozen raw? Or should you be making your own pet food at home? Determining the best diet may seem overwhelming, but it doesn't have to be. In this chapter, we'll discuss some of the options and the factors to consider when making your decision. Let's begin with three major facts about food options that you should know.

Feeding a high-quality commercial diet is OK. Commercial pet food is far from perfect, but the best brands do provide very good, nutritionally complete diets for companion animals. So if you prefer feeding your animals such a diet, it is fine.

Supplementing can make a healthier diet. Supplementing your pet's diet with appropriate fresh, chemical-free whole food will make your companion animal's diet even healthier.

Making your own pet food is not that complicated. Some people (such as the owners of dog food companies) would like you to believe that making your own pet food is too complicated. In reality, you can do it successfully—as long as you know what your animal needs. You can't just give him a bowl of ground hamburger and keep him healthy.

As for the eco-conscious aspect of food, here are three more points to consider when making your decision.

Organically produced food is better for the environment. Even if studies haven't definitively proven that it is nutritionally superior (although recent studies suggest it might be), organic food, whether marketed for animals or humans, is produced without chemicals that can pollute the groundwater and the air. Animals raised for organic meat must, by law, be humanely treated and fed organic feed. Thus you may consider organically produced food a more eco-friendly and humane choice.

Locally produced foods are better than shipped foods. Local food doesn't need as many preserving agents because it doesn't have to travel as far before consumption, and that shorter travel time also translates to less energy and pollution from transportation. The more local food, the better.

Certain companies are eco-conscious in the manufacturing of their products. Environmentally conscious food companies may use alternative energy sources such as wind or solar power, may choose sustainable and/or locally produced ingredients, and may be packaged in recycled and/or recyclable packaging, or in packaging made with sustainable materials. To make a

Green Facts

Organic foods are grown without the use of chemical pesticides, artificial fertilizers, or any kind of sewage. They may not be genetically modified or irradiated and may not be processed with any artificial additives other than those on a short government-approved list. Animals processed into organic meat must be treated according to humane standards and fed only organic feed. Because organic farms tend to be smaller (although this isn't always true) and because they are chemical free, they are better for the environment.

more eco-conscious choice, seek out those companies.

That's the short version, but let's look at each of these elements a little more closely.

Pet Food: The Out-of-the-Bag Diet

Feeding conventional pet food to your companion animals seems a lot cheaper than paying top dollar for super-premium food made in small batches from organic ingredients. And it is by far less time consuming than making pet food at home. For many of us, it's hard to let go of cost and convenience. Besides, what if your dog *likes* his cheap kibble?

However, if you look at what is really going on beyond the simple price tag comparison, you will quickly discover that eating green can be not only better for you, your family, and the earth but also *less* expensive, depending on how you go about it. In addition, while dollars and cents matter to all of us, especially in these economically challenging times, the big picture may grow in your mind to include important health concerns, ethical considerations, and matters of personal responsibility. Let's consider what your animal companions are eating.

Pet Food History

People have been feeding animals for thousands of years without the benefit of bags of packaged kibble. Commercial pet food is a relatively new phenomenon, making its appearance just over a hundred years ago, first as pet treats and then pet food. The convenience appealed to busy Americans,

Green Facts

Currently, pet food using the term **organic** on the label must follow the same regulations human food does. If a food claims to be organic, it must contain at least 95 percent organic ingredients. If it claims to be "made with organic ingredients," it must contain at least 70 percent organic ingredients. However, enforcement of organic label claims on pet foods isn't necessarily a priority for many states, and the current details of organic regulations don't always fit the needs of pet food manufacturers. To help correct the situation, the National Organic Standards Board, part of the USDA, organized an Organic Pet Food Task Force to make recommendations for new regulations that would apply specifically to organic pet food. These recommendations are now in place, but they have not yet become law. Keep track of developments on the Organic Trade Association Web site: www.ota.com.

even in the early 1900s. The first treats were a mixture of grains, vegetables, and meat, and the first canned pet food was made out of horse meat. Pet food soon became a convenient way to dispose of meat and meat by-products (other parts of the animal, such as organs, bones, tendons, and skin) that humans wouldn't or couldn't eat, and the industry thrived. Canned cat food appeared in the 1930s. The process for producing dry kibble was invented in the 1950s. By the mid-twentieth century, pet food had become a $200 million industry.

By the 1980s, pet food manufacturers had begun to diversify with different formulas, and a few companies started to question the quality of pet food and the effect it might be having on pets. Premium foods began to appear, advertising higher-quality ingredients rather than the throwaway ingredients of pet foods past. Pet food is a multibillion-dollar industry today, offering consumers a wide range of foods, of differing quality, from cheap to high end. Some foods are formulated for puppies, kittens, overweight pets, active working dogs, or pets with certain health problems such as diabetes, kidney disease, and even canine dementia. Some foods contain ingredients to support joint health, a healthier skin and coat, and better digestion. Antioxidants, essential fatty acids, and organic ingredients also now appear in many foods. Some companies tout the use of whole grains, while others proudly proclaim they are grain free.

Many of these foods give animals excellent nutrition—others, not so much. It's mostly a matter of ingredient quality. But then there is the contamination factor.

Pet Food Problems and Improvements

In spring 2007, many brands of dry and canned cat and dog food were recalled when they were found to be tainted with poisonous melamine. (Melamine, not a legal food ingredient, makes foods appear to contain more protein than they actually do, so it was added illegally to meet required protein levels for less cost.) The melamine was traced to wheat gluten from China. As a result of eating the contaminated food, thousands of cats and dogs sickened, and some died.

The FDA and the USDA investigated, and in February 2008, two Chinese nationals and the businesses that they operate as well as an American company and its president and CEO were all "indicted by a federal grand jury for their role in a scheme to import products purported to be wheat gluten into the United States that were contaminated with melamine," according to the FDA.

Since then, we've seen not only pet food but also infant formula and other milk products from China adulterated with melamine. As of this writing, four children have died after ingesting the tainted products, and more than 50,000 people—many of them children—suffered kidney stones and other health problems from the melamine. Then there were pretzels and candy and other foodstuffs found to be tainted.

The recall and the subsequent food scandals were a wake-up call for many people who had always assumed that if food came in a package from the store, it had to be safe. This event triggered a sea change in the pet food industry because suddenly people wanted to know not only what was in pet food but also where the ingredients came from and whether they

were actually beneficial. Pet foods, already being improved, began to change more rapidly and dramatically. Several companies stopped using wheat gluten, then wheat altogether, since some animals don't digest wheat very well. Other fillers started to drop out of commercial foods as well. Some brands of pet food have gotten better as a result of this unfortunate experience.

However, some people still don't trust commercial pet food. Others believe that unprocessed organic whole food is the only natural diet for an animal, so let's examine

that claim and what a natural diet for a wild animal really is.

The Natural Diet

The notion that wild animals eat some kind of perfect diet specifically formulated and served up by mother nature isn't necessarily true. Animals in the wild sometimes suffer from food poisoning, nutritional deficiencies, and even starvation. As one veterinary nutritionist told me, "Wild animals eat what they can find." They may be eating a *natural* diet, but that doesn't mean they are eating the best possible foods for their health.

In addition, although wild canines have evolved strong digestive systems over the millennia and can survive on a lot of junk, including the garbage discarded by humans, many domesticated pets have lost the ability to digest what their wild counterparts can endure. Domestic dogs also have teeth less conditioned to chewing bones, making some dogs prone to dental fractures. Clearly, our domestic animals need more specific considerations than wolves and coyotes do, especially since they can't fend for themselves.

If you combine elements of your animal companion's natural diet—such as fresh organic meat—with carefully formulated high-quality commercial pet food (dry, canned, or frozen raw), you can feel good about doing the best for your companion animals and the planet.

The Homemade Diet

We feed our animals, so it's up to us to do a good job, not poison them with chemicals. That notion has sent a lot of people to their own cupboards and refrigerators, seeking out homemade food they can prepare for their pets, just so they can be sure it is safe. I've been writing about pet food for years now, and I've interviewed numerous veterinarians and canine nutritionists on the subject. It turns out that, generally, the food that is best for animal (and human) health is also best for the health of the planet: fresh food produced locally without chemicals and consumed close to the time that it was harvested.

But how do you do that with your companion animals? Some people say that making pet food at home is easy and feeding pets isn't that different from feeding kids. Others vehemently disagree, saying that you can create serious nutritional deficiencies in your pets if you don't know what you are doing. In my experience, different animals thrive on different kinds of diets, and to some extent you have to figure out what works best for *your* pet. However, in general, one way to improve your pet's diet is to introduce some of the healthy, eco-conscious foods *you* eat. However, you must make certain first that those foods are actually good for the animal you are feeding and that they are served only in the right proportions. Some foods can hurt dogs, such as onions and garlic, grapes, raisins, chocolate, alcohol, and caffeine. Dogs also need to absorb all of the essential major and minor nutrients in the right proportions. Some protein sources, for example, are better absorbed than others.

Cats have a less varied diet, requiring a greater percentage of meat than dogs, and most veterinarians agree cats cannot thrive on a vegetarian diet. However, cats don't just eat the prey's muscle meat. They eat the whole animal. Likewise, they can enjoy a variety of foods, as long as the nutritional proportions are correct for their species.

Realize that making pet food at home isn't for everyone. Do you have time to cook dinner for the human members of your family as well as a separate dinner for the animals? If you decide to make your own pet food at home, you will need to do some research beyond the scope of this book.

Remember that many sources, especially on the Internet, have a vested interest in selling something, so look for objective information from unbiased authorities.

There are good books out there that will tell you how to feed your pet a homemade diet or supplement with homemade treats. I like these books (but talk to your veterinarian to make sure you are giving your pets everything they need nutritionally):

Dr. Pitcairn's New Complete Guide to Natural Health for Dogs and Cats, by Richard H. Pitcairn and Susan Hubble Pitcairn, Rodale Books, 2005.

Real Food for Dogs: 50 Vet-Approved Recipes to Please the Canine Gastronome, by Arden Moore, Storey Publishing, 2001.

The Ultimate Dog Treat Cookbook: Homemade Goodies for Man's Best Friend, by Liz Palika, Howell Book House, 2005.

The Whole Pet Diet: Eight Weeks to Great Health for Dogs and Cats, by Andi Brown, Celestial Arts, 2006.

🔥 Although it focuses on treats rather than on a complete diet, I can't leave off my own book, full of fun-to-make, homey recipes for dogs: *Chowhound Dog Treat Baking Book*, Sterling, 2009.

I admit I do not feed my own pets an exclusively homemade diet. Instead, I follow a more moderate route—the complementary diet.

The Complementary Diet

An easier option for most people is to feed their companion animals the highest quality commercial diet they can find and supplement that diet with up to 25 percent fresh, nutritionally appropriate whole food, such as fresh meat, poultry, fish, and, in the case of dogs, whole grains and ground vegetables. This is what I do to ensure that my own companion animals get all the nutrition they need but also benefit from whole foods. Sally's favorite meal is a small scoop of kibble mixed with a little spaghetti and meat sauce (hold the onions), just like

in the love scene in the Disney movie *Lady and the Tramp.* Combining premium natural kibble with healthy "people" food is an easy way to make your companion animal's diet both nutritious and eco-friendlier.

To do this, begin by choosing several good pet foods and alternate them so your companion animal gets a more varied diet. The best choices contain ingredients you recognize. If you don't know what an ingredient is or if it sounds like it isn't food, then it probably isn't an environmentally friendly or particularly healthful ingredient. Long chemical names sometimes are vitamins or minerals, but the label should identify them as such for you.

Be sure also to choose a prepared diet that is nutritionally suitable for your companion animal. Healthier animals are much more enjoyable companions, and you'll pay less money at the veterinarian's office. Dog food can contain a variety of ingredients but should be composed mostly of high-quality protein sources and very little, if any, cheap processed grain. Small amounts of whole grains are fine for most dogs. Cat food diets should contain little to no grain.

Consider picking a prepared diet that uses mostly organic ingredients. If the food says it is an organic food, it must consist of at least 95 percent organic ingredients. If it says "made with organic ingredients," the percentages can be lower. Organic ingredients are produced without environmentally damaging chemicals and must meet humane standards for animal care.

Other suggestions for how choosing the right packaged foods and being eco-conscious are listed below.

Avoid foods that list "by-products" in the ingredients. In commercial pet food, the term *by-products* is vague, and manufacturers don't have to reveal what exactly those by-products are. For this reason, many people choose to avoid pet foods that contain by-products. The inclusion of organ meat, when described as such on the label, is good.

Choose ingredients sourced in the United States. Choose a prepared diet that uses ingredients sourced in the United States, rather than shipped from foreign countries at great energy cost. Companies will expend less energy shipping food to local stores.

Contact the pet food companies for information. Ask whether the company is eco-conscious. Does it make pet health and green manufacturing a priority? What are the company's environmental initiatives? Companies that are eco-conscious should be only too happy to share their efforts with you when you ask.

To help you further in deciding which foods to choose for your companion animal, I have listed in the Resources section of this book the pet food and treat companies that have particularly impressed me with their commitment to animal health, the highest quality ingredients, and/or the environment.

Next, add healthy, whole food.

The Share-the-Love-and-the-Dinner Diet

Many of the healthful, environmentally friendly food *you* eat can be fine for your companion animal and in fact might be the

nutritional spark he needs to thrive. Commercial pet food is highly processed, but real, fresh whole food is better for you and better for your animal.

Some eco-friendly choices for supplementing your companion animal's diet include the following foods:

Fresh organic chicken, turkey, duck, and rabbit, preferably free-range or cage-free, including organ meats such as chicken livers and gizzards

Organic cage-free eggs

Green Fact

Dogs are omnivores, like humans, and in the wild survive on a very wide variety of foods. In other words, dogs can get by. They can even be vegetarians, if their diets are carefully planned.

Fresh wild-caught fish, such as salmon

Small bits of fresh organic fruit, such as blueberries and apples

Small amounts of well-cooked whole grains, particularly oatmeal and barley

Finely chopped and/or cooked and mashed vegetables, like green peas, sweet potatoes, carrots, green beans, and squash

Any combination foods (like soups, stews, or casseroles) that you are eating, as long as they only contain safe, healthy ingredients for your animal. Avoid onions!

A small amount of oil containing essential fatty acids can be drizzled on your

> There is not one world for man and one for animals; they are part of the same one and lead parallel lives.
>
> —Rigoberta Menchú,
> Guatemalan Indian writer, activist, and Nobel Peace Prize winner (1992)

pet's foods. Good choices for pets (and people) include cod liver or other fish oil, flax seed oil, hemp oil, extra virgin olive oil, soybean oil, and canola oil.

The Raw Diet

In the wild, dogs and cats eat a lot of raw meat, including organs, some bone, and in some cases, the small amount of digested plant material in the stomach contents of the small prey. For this reason, many people choose to feed their dogs and cats a diet of raw meat and bone with a small amount of well-ground vegetables. For dogs, some people also include cooked whole grains (cats are more carnivorous than dogs and in most cases should not eat grains). Many companion animals do extremely well on this kind of diet.

But preparing a raw diet for a dog or a cat isn't for every person, and not every animal does well on it. This kind of diet also remains controversial. As discussed previously, our domesticated animals often don't have the digestion or the teeth for a raw diet. Additionally, although dogs and cats typically tolerate food that would make a human ill, some still do get sick from pathogens in raw meat, such as salmonella. The greater worry, however, is that humans—particularly children—exposed to the dog's or cat's raw meat diet will get sick from those pathogens.

That doesn't mean your companion animal can't eat a better diet. You can feed raw food carefully, or you can cook for all of your family members, no matter what species. Commercially prepared frozen raw diets can make feeding raw relatively easy.

The Vegetarian Diet

Many people who choose a vegetarian lifestyle don't want any meat in their homes and feed their dogs vegetarian diets, too. Some dogs do just fine on these diets, while others do poorly and will enjoy better health on a diet that includes meat. Most vegetarian pet foods, such as those produced by PetGuard, are nutritionally complete. If you choose such a diet for your dog, keep an eye on his weight and general condition to be sure he is thriving.

Cats, being obligate carnivores, cannot thrive on a vegetarian diet. Some people say they feed their cats this way, but to stay healthy, these cats would need complex supplementation, including the essential acid taurine. None of the veterinarians I have interviewed on the subject say they would feed cats a vegetarian diet, but talk to your own veterinarian if you want to investigate this idea further.

Your Diet

I would feel remiss, in a book about eco-conscious living, if I didn't mention what the people in the house might want to consider doing with their own diets. It would be silly to invest your resources in an environmentally sound and healthful diet for your pets and not do the same thing for your family and yourself.

For some people, refusing to eat animal products is the natural answer to the quest to live in greater harmony with the earth. If you love animals and you want to live a greener life, the arguments for a meat-free diet are compelling. Conventional meat production is one of the biggest sources of pollution on the planet as well as a source of much animal cruelty. Many people thrive on a vegetarian or vegan diet (no animal products of any kind, including dairy prod-

ucts) and believe this is an important way to live. For others, vegetarianism does not work so well. Some people say that they do poorly, feel ill, or just do not enjoy eating that way.

However, there are ways to consume meat in an eco-friendlier way. If you don't want to go meat free, at least consider these environmentally beneficial actions.

Choose locally produced, organic meat. According to the Natural Resources Defense Council, factory farms produce huge amounts of animal waste that often leak or overflow into public water supplies, tainting our water with, among other things, pathogens such as drug-resistant bacteria. Cows, pigs, and even chickens (stacked in tiny cages) crowded into factory farms produce toxic gases such as ammonia and methane and often live in horrifying conditions. Every year, factory farms generate more pollution than all the cars driving in the United States. If you choose to eat meat, it makes sense to eat less of it, and the eco-friendly choice is to buy and eat locally produced meat, preferably organic, from small family farms.

Buy wild-caught, sustainable fish. According to the Organic Consumers Association, fish farming also produces huge amounts of pollutants that can harm both humans and the environment (not to mention the fish). Farmed salmon are typically vaccinated to survive in crowded, disease-ridden conditions and dyed pink so they look more like our idea of salmon. Wild-caught, sustainably fished seafood is a better choice. To help select sustainable fish sources, get the *Pocket Seafood Selector*, www.edf.org/documents/1980_pocket_seafood_selector.pdf, published by the Environmental Defense Fund. Or try the *Sustainable Seafood Guide* on the Earth Easy Web site, www.eartheasy.com/eat_sustainable_seafoods.htm.

Buy organic milk. Other countries do not permit the use of bovine growth hormone (BGH), but in the United States, dairies often give this to their cows because it results in a greater volume of milk. According to the USDA, BGH is safe, but many people disagree. If you'd rather not risk it, or don't like supporting milk superproduction via chemicals, buy organic milk.

Go as organic as possible. Organic whole grains, vegetables, and fruits not only mean you consume fewer pesticides but that fewer chemicals were used in the production of those foods, and that's better

for the environment, too. Organic farming is a growing industry, so it's easier than ever before to go organic. And organic produce tastes better, in my opinion.

If you alter the diets of your animal companions to be eco-friendlier, I hope you will alter your own as well, in whatever way makes sense to you. If you care about combating the cruelty so often involved in the mass production of meat, eggs, and dairy products; avoiding the chemicals humans and animals ingest when they eat the meat of other exposed animals; and not filling up the world with factory farm waste, then I hope you will consider acting on your beliefs.

You can do so by reducing or eliminating meat and dairy consumption, or by purchasing the meat and dairy products you do choose to eat from local family farms practicing organic methods. It can mean all the difference to your own health, your conscience, and the earth.

Chapter 3

Altered
States

Spay/Neuter

Matters

Love is not love which alters when it alteration finds." When Shakespeare penned these words (in sonnet 116), he probably wasn't thinking about his dog or even the feral cats prowling the streets of London. However, let's consider the quote completely out of context. If you spay (for females) or neuter (for males)**

your dog, cat, or rabbit, then your companion animal cannot make more puppies, kittens, and bunnies. Will that cause you to love your pet any less? Of course not.

In Jack's case, that's a very good thing. My little blond Pomeranian-terrier mix is a bundle of genetic health problems. At the tender age of two, he came down with glaucoma and now has to have very

expensive eye drops administered daily. He also has luxating patellas—kneecaps that slip out of place—and allergies that make him wheeze and cough frequently. He has suffered from unexplained temporary rear-limb paralysis that lasted for two days and then disappeared as quickly as it came, and he is an obsessive-compulsive licker. I love him and he's really, really cute, but

From 2 to 80 Million

According to the American Humane Association, if two cats and their surviving offspring were to breed freely for ten years, producing two litters per year with 2 to 3 kittens surviving from each litter, they would produce more than 80 million cats.

would I want him to lend his faulty genes to future generations? No way.

Even when a pet is sound, healthy, and gorgeous, do you really want to be responsible for producing more companion animals in a world that already can't take care of all the ones it has? Your veterinarian encourages spaying or neutering your companion animal, and shelters, rescue groups, and in many cases breeders require it. Your companion animal will enjoy better health. *And* it's better for the environment.

But Isn't It Unnatural?

If you love and respect the natural world and you love and respect your companion animals, then you probably want your animals to live a natural life. You want them to be the animals they are, with all

their parts intact. So why would you subject them to surgery that renders them sterile? It just seems so *unnatural* to remove a female cat's uterus or a male dog's testicles, right? Ouch.

I get it, and this feeling is perfectly legitimate. Spaying or neutering your pet *is* unnatural, but you could also argue that *having* a pet is unnatural, as is feeding a cat processed kibble or letting a dog sleep in your bed.

Sure, the idea of sterilizing a family member may seem harsh, but in reality, it's not. The surgery, performed under anesthesia by a licensed veterinarian, is simple,

Green Guidance

Some female birds begin to lay eggs even if they don't have another bird partner, because they bond so strongly with their human companions. However, laying eggs can put a bird's health at risk by depleting her of nutrients and predisposing her to osteoporosis and other problems such as becoming eggbound (when the egg gets stuck inside the bird). It is a good idea to discourage egg-laying behavior, for the health and safety of your bird companion. Here's how:

- Don't let your bird spend too much time in the dark. Dark spaces encourage egg-laying behavior.
- Don't let your bird stay up all night. Put her to bed when the sun goes down.
- If your bird seems unusually attached to a particular toy, take it away. It can get her excited enough to start laying eggs.
- Be sure your bird gets exposure to sunlight and eats a complete, healthy diet.
- If your bird does lay an egg, don't take it away. If you take it away, she might be encouraged to lay another.

For more information, talk to a veterinarian with experience in avian medicine. You can find one at the Association of Avian Veterinarians: www.aav.org/vet-lookup.

and recovery time is quick. Your pet may be groggy for a few hours afterward and you'll want to keep an eye on the stitches, but a spay/neuter surgery is a common procedure and your veterinarian has probably done it many, many times.

It isn't the surgery that is harsh. It is the fact that there are homeless companion animals being euthanized by the millions because there aren't enough homes for them all. We created this problem by bringing animals into our homes as pets, so it is our responsibility, as the guardians of our animal companions, to do everything we can to make the situation right. Spaying or neutering pets is an effective solution. If everyone without intentions to breed

healthy, sound animals with good temperaments had their companion animals spayed or neutered, shelters might have to close down. I'm fairly certain everybody would be OK with that.

Fortunately, because so many shelters, breeders, and even pet stores have widely publicized spay/neuter campaigns, the effort has already made a difference. According to some sources, up to 75 percent of dogs have already been spayed or neutered. Shelters are far less crowded than they once were and they euthanize fewer animals than they once did. Responsible pet owners know they should spay or neuter their pets, and most of them do so, at least eventually.

But maybe you're thinking it would be fun to breed your dog or cat. Wouldn't the puppies or kittens be so adorable? Of course they would, but then what? Are you going to keep all the offspring, or are you going to find homes for them? Once they go to someone else's home, you've lost control over the situation. If the person who adopts the puppy or kitten you allowed to be created can't handle the responsibility or experiences a change of circumstances, that puppy or kitten could end up in a shelter, and chances are good that the shelter will be the end of the line. That's *definitely* unnatural.

Maybe you don't intend to breed your pet. Great! Breeding should be left to people who are committed to learning everything they can about that art and science.

Green Fact

The last Tuesday of February is Spay Day USA, a campaign sponsored by the Humane Society of the United States to raise awareness about the importance of spaying or neutering pets and feral cats.

However, accidents happen. The one time your dog gets out might be the one time he impregnates the neighbor's unspayed dog. The one time your female cat gets out might be the one time she comes home pregnant. Now you've got more unwanted animals in need of homes.

Consider this as well: if your pet does have a litter and you do find a home for all those puppies or kittens, think about how many homes you've used up, homes that might have been available for a few of the millions of dogs and cats already waiting in animal shelters. Those people may not go

Green Facts

There are several myths about the consequences of spaying or neutering. Here are the facts:

Fact: Spaying or neutering does not make pets fatter and lazier.

Fact: Allowing your female dog or cat to have a litter is not healthier for her.

Fact: Spaying or neutering does not reduce a dog's protective instinct.

Fact: Neutering often reduces an animal's desire to wander and may also decrease spraying and marking behavior inside the house.

Green Tip

In an effort to promote spaying and neutering, many shelters and even some pet stores offer coupons for free or greatly reduced spaying or neutering that you can use with local veterinarians. Ask your veterinarian about ways to reduce the cost. Remember that unlike checkups, food, grooming, and other ongoing costs, a spaying or neutering procedure is a one-time cost, with benefits that will last a lifetime.

to the shelter because they got a puppy or a kitten from you.

Euthanizing millions of dogs and cats certainly isn't "natural," and preventing the production of more puppies and kittens can help prevent this unnatural situation. No matter how you look at it, the problem of pet overpopulation and euthanasia is a strong argument for spaying or neutering your pet.

The Health Question

If you spay or neuter your companion animal, he or she not only will never reproduce more unwanted animals but also will enjoy better health—a great perk. Studies show that spayed female dogs have a much lower incidence of uterine infections and

cancer of the reproductive organs, such as the ovaries and breasts. Neutered male dogs also have fewer problems related to their sexual organs. They can't get testicular cancer, and they have far fewer prostate problems. Spayed and neutered pets live longer, too.

However, some research suggests that sterilization can contribute to other health problems, such as thyroid problems, joint disease, and certain types of cancer, such as osteosarcoma (bone cancer) and hemangiosarcoma (tumor of the blood vessels). Although researchers have differing points of view on the subject, the benefits of spaying for female dogs seem to outweigh the risks, while with male dogs, neutering seems to prevent about as many health problems as it could cause.

Because there is little compelling reason *not* to spay or neuter dogs or cats, and many social and humane reasons why spaying or neutering is a good idea, most veterinarians recommend it. However, the jury is still out on whether spaying or neutering at an early age (prior to four months) will cause future health problems. In general, most veterinarians recommend spaying or neutering after six months of age. Just be sure nobody gets pregnant before that time! Pets can reach sexual maturity before six months.

Other Benefits

The procedure also benefits you and your peaceful home environment. Unspayed female dogs will go into heat when they reach sexual maturity, and that can get

Green Words

messy because they menstruate. You will have to deal with towels and pads, or deal with bloodstains on your carpet. Unneutered male dogs and cats are more likely to roam and seek out females in heat, behave aggressively, and spray and mark in the house. Most of the wandering dogs that bite people and get hit by cars are unneutered males. Unneutered male cats allowed to wander are also most likely to get hit by cars or injured in cat fights.

Spayed and neutered animals tend to behave more agreeably, especially if they are altered before reaching sexual maturity (one argument for earlier spaying/neutering). They will be less likely to wander off, get into fights, be aggressive, spray in the house, or get all worked up when a dog in heat or a yowling male cat shows up outside the window (and if your pet is spayed or neutered, those other animals probably won't show up outside the window anyway).

Why Spay/Neuter Is Greener

Too many unwanted pets mean not only more euthanasia (and its resulting terrible waste in landfills) but more wandering stray animals. Shelters are reporting unprecedented numbers of stray pets picked up on the streets, and many people theorize that a poor economy has forced owners to abandon the pets that they can no longer afford to feed. What are all those strays doing to the planet?

Stray dogs and cats are responsible for their own brand of environmental destruction. They prey on local wildlife, knock over trash cans, and spread bacteria into our environment from their urine and feces, polluting the soil and the groundwater with potentially dangerous pathogens that can affect other animals and people. Sometimes they fight with pets or even bite humans. Spaying or neutering your own pets guarantees you won't add to any of these problems.

But, to take the argument to the next level, the basic humane nature of spaying or neutering your companion animal is also greener because it is an act that respects the earth and respects animals. When you have a veterinarian spay or neuter your companion animal, you are stepping up to your responsibility as a steward of the natural world, doing what is best for the health and welfare of the nonhuman members of your family. So be green by making sure

Green Guidance

You've heard the expression "breed like bunnies," so you probably know that rabbits are very, um . . . prolific. Can you really spay or neuter a rabbit? Is it necessary? Actually, it is. Rabbits will produce bunnies if you have a male/female pair. Even if you don't, rabbits that have been spayed or neutered tend to be calmer and more affectionate, enjoying human companionship more. They also enjoy a reduced risk of reproductive cancers and tend to live longer and fight less with other animals. Spayed or neutered rabbits have better litter habits and seem to learn better. Plus, you can get a friend for your bunny and not worry about ending up with a hundred more! For more information on spaying or neutering rabbits and the associated risks (which are small), visit the House Rabbit Society Web site at www.rabbit.org.

your companion animals can't accidentally reproduce. You'll not only be reducing your own pets' carbon pawprints, but you won't be producing any additional unwanted pawprints, either.

What about Spay/ Neuter Laws?

If spaying and neutering pets is so great, shouldn't the law make them mandatory? In fact, some areas do have such laws, but they are controversial. Typically, they require all pet owners to spay or neuter their dogs and cats or risk being fined a hefty sum. Anyone who does not want to spay or neuter a dog or cat, such as a small hobby breeder, must pay a fee or buy a license to breed.

That may sound sensible on the surface. However, many of the laws exempt large breeding operations even though these operations probably contribute significantly to the problem of pet overpopulation. Small, responsible hobby breeders likely do not contribute to the problem but would have to bear the financial burden. These are the same breeders who don't profit from their efforts and often don't have a lot of extra financial resources to spare. Obviously, this is not fair.

Such laws are extremely difficult to enforce, and the people least likely to comply with the law are probably the ones most likely to let their pets breed indiscriminately. Those who are likely to comply, such as hobby breeders who don't want their reputations ruined, are the least likely to behave irresponsibly.

In addition, some people see the law as an infringement on their rights and believe people should make the decision for their own animals. They may choose not to have their animals sterilized, but they will also try to manage their animals in a way that ensures (of course, there are no guarantees) they won't reproduce.

Regardless of whether such laws exist where you live and whether you support or oppose them, the simple fact is that for most pet owners, spaying or neutering makes good sense all around. Do it of your own volition, and you won't have to worry, law or no law. It all comes down to being greener, kinder, and more aware. Spaying or neutering your companion animal is the right thing to do.

Chapter 4

Nipping
Pet-Sumerism

How Much Stuff
Does Your Pet
Really Need?

Let's talk about shopping. More specifically, let's talk about pet-sumerism. The pet product industry produces more today than it ever has, and it continues to grow. In 1998, people in the United States spent $23 billion on pet products. In 2008, they spent more than $43 billion, according to statistics that were compiled by

the American Pet Products Association. How much we spend on our pets directly reflects how much we care about them.

Or does it?

In an era in which consumerism drives the economy, it can be easy to feel justified in spending a lot of money. Through advertising in various media, profit-driven corporate America constantly sends out the message that spending is good, that we *must* spend to help our country, that we *need* the next new thing. And isn't spending money *fun*? It's fun to get new stuff. It's a rush. Almost an addiction. We are a culture of consumerists. Isn't that what America is all about?

Your companion animal might just beg to differ.

Green Facts

According to a 2008 United Nations report titled **Atmospheric Brown Clouds**, pollution from automobiles, deforestation for agriculture, fires, and coal-fired power plants have created "brown clouds" in the atmosphere that have blotted out the light over much of southern Africa, the Amazon basin, North America, and especially Asia. A November 2008 issue of the **New York Times** reported that clouds have diminished sunlight to such an extent that crop yields in rural India have decreased. According to scientists, the swath of brown haze is more than a mile thick and spans much of the sky from the Arabian Peninsula to the Yellow Sea, sometimes drifting all the way to California. The United Nations report named thirteen cities as most plagued by the brown clouds, including Bangkok, Cairo, New Delhi, Seoul, and Tehran. Approximately 340,000 people in China and India die every year from cardiovascular and respiratory diseases related to air pollution.

I believe that in many regards, animals and children are alike, especially in that they don't really want all of that stuff. What they really want is *you*—your time, your energy, your affection, your attention. It has nothing to do with money, spending, or buying stuff. Maybe it's about time that we nipped pet-sumerism in the bud.

Let's think about the environmental impact of all that stuff companion animals don't need. Think of the packaging thrown away. The Environmental Protection Agency says Americans throw away 220 million tons of garbage a year. Think about the gas you use to get back and forth to the store.

And what about the product's *embodied energy*? Even if you ordered all that "stuff" online, how much energy did it take to produce it, and how much did it take to get it to you? How much energy will you expend using it and disposing of it? What about all of the pollution produced during that process?

Now think about what your pet gets out of all that stuff. Does he care that his toy is high tech, or would he just as soon have a tennis ball and someone to throw it? Does he truly need that dog sweater, that fancy collar, those booties, another new bed, the multiple bowls, and the leashes in every possible color?

Our companion animals do need certain items, and many other products can benefit them even if they aren't absolutely essential.

Your dog might not need a bed because he would rather sleep with you, or he might not need a new bed right now, but he might benefit from a dog sweater if he has

Green Words

a thin, fine coat and really does get cold outside. Your cat might not need twenty-seven catnip toys, but he might benefit from one or two, plus a really good scratching post, to keep him busy and away from the back of the couch. (That benefits *you* and

Green Words

the environment—you won't have to buy another couch!)

Our animal companions are fairly lucky these days. Many of the items that they need, as well as ones that can benefit them, are more widely available and affordable than ever before. And yet many of us do spend too much money, sometimes out of guilt for not spending enough time with our pets, or just because we like to buy things, or because we think of them as our children and we also buy our kids too much stuff.

But think of the price we all pay when we spend too much time, energy, and resources on living the life of a consumer. We lose focus, missing out on the simpler pleasures of life that don't cost anything, like spending time with our families, playing outside, and going on walks.

We fritter away our bank accounts and often find ourselves stuck when an emergency expense comes up, wondering where all our money went. We spend more time shopping, and working to support all that shopping, and less time doing the things we actually enjoy, things that are fulfilling and meaningful and that stick with us.

In this chapter, you'll find some basic guidelines for helping you decide whether you should buy something, based on some basic tenets of simple living. At the end of this chapter, look for ten earth-friendly criteria that you can apply to any potential purchase to help you determine whether the environmental impact is worth the price. Then you can shop, maybe not until you drop, but at least with a clearer conscience.

Questions to Ask before Buying

You want it. You might even need it. But before you buy it, ask yourself three important questions. These questions will help you to stop, breathe, and think before making an impulse purchase. They will also help you clarify your goals and priorities. The questions are: Why am I buying this? What else could I do with the money? And, what's really important here? Let's look at each one.

Why Buy?

Before you buy any new product for your companion animal (or even for yourself), ask yourself this question: Why am I buying this? You might be able to break down the question even further. Consider:

- Does somebody in my family really need this?
- Does somebody really need this today? It is something that genuinely cannot

wait until next week, next month, or even next year?

    🔥 Am I certain that I don't already have one of these items at home?

    🔥 Am I sure it wouldn't be better to repair something I already have at home rather than buy this?

    🔥 Can I afford this?

Asking yourself these questions not only helps you put your tendency to shop into perspective but also forces you to stop and think before you whip out that credit card. That alone could save you a lot of money

as well as save the earth from the burden of a lot of extra trash. If you don't know the answer or you can't give yourself a good answer, take a deep breath and hold off on the purchase. Do it for mother earth.

What Else Could I Do with the Money?

Simple-living advocates often encourage people to look at their money in terms of life energy. If you have the urge to buy something, consider how much life energy you invested to earn the money you would

> *An honest man is one who knows that he can't consume more than he has produced.*
>
> —Ayn Rand,
> author, *Atlas Shrugged*

spend on that item. Is it worth that price in sweat and tears and time? What else could you do with the money you are thinking about spending on another dog toy or those fancy gourmet treats? Could you buy something you need or want more? Could you buy something your dog needs or wants more? Could you save it so you can retire sooner and spend more time at home with your pets?

Question every purchase, big and small. Get in the habit, and I can almost guarantee you'll start spending less and saving more. Because in the end, it's about what's important.

What's Important?

Every time you buy something, you become further enmeshed in a cycle of consumerism that can be hard to escape. The more stuff you have, the more time it takes to maintain it, the more space you need to store it, and the more resources you need just to use it, including bringing it home, showing it to others, and eventually disposing of it. A bigger house costs more and takes more time to clean. More cars cost more, pollute more, and take more to maintain. More clothes require more resources to produce them, more energy to wash them, and more time deciding which ones to wear. And more pet stuff? Are you sure your dog or cat or rabbit or bird wouldn't rather just spend more time with you? The more you buy and the more you have, the more you have to work to afford it all, and that means less time just *being*. Ask your pets which they'd prefer: more stuff or more you at home, just *being*. They can show you how. Watch your pets for a while, and you might begin to understand the rationale. The way I see it, the more stuff you have, the less *you* you have, and the less stuff you have, the more freedom you get.

Green Term

Embodied energy is a term for all the energy a product will use during its manufacture, sale, use, and disposal.

Sustainable and Renewable

If you decide that you really do need to buy something, hold off just another few minutes. There are more things to consider if you want to be a truly green consumer. One of the first questions you need to answer is: Is that product sustainable and renewable?

Sustainable and renewable materials are those that can easily be replaced without harm to the environment. For example, materials such as hemp and bamboo are renewable because they grow so quickly. Cut them down to use in products, and it does not take long to grow more. Hardwood, by contrast, is not as renewable because it can take a tree many decades to grow. However, if it is only harvested at the rate that it grows, it can be sustainable.

Sustainable materials are easy to grow without a lot of chemical intervention. If a particular plant doesn't need pesticide because it is a native crop adapted to the local climate, it is more sustainable than a delicate nonnative plant that requires a lot of pesticide and fertilizer to keep it alive. If a crop that is normally heavily sprayed is grown organically (like cotton), that's also sustainable because it doesn't degrade the environment.

In addition, native or local materials are more sustainable than are imported materials. They require less fuel to transport and less time to get to their location, so their harvest, processing, and shipping are more efficient. In other words, sustainable and renewable products are made in a way that does not degrade the environment or does not use up the materials it requires faster than they can be replaced.

Organic and Sustainable Cotton

Cotton sounds like a natural, renewable fiber, but in reality, according to the eco-

Green Guidance

Organic fabric is great in general but not when it is treated with toxic dyes. According to Pam Wheelock, the founder and owner of Purrfectplay, processed cotton cloth has typically been treated with chlorine, formaldehyde, and phenols, all known toxins. Fabric dyes can contain arsenic, lead, cadmium, cobalt, and chromium. Undyed organic cotton costs more than conventional cotton, but if you figure in the possible hazards of conventional cotton, the cost doesn't seem like such a big deal. For more on the toxic nature of fabrics and fabric dyes, check out Purrfectplay's informative Web site at www.purrfectplay.com, and sign up for its newsletter.

friendly folks at Purrfectplay, a small pet toy company in Indiana, most of the 12 million acres of cotton grown in the United States every year is heavily sprayed with pesticides, to the tune of 8.5 million tons a year. Because cotton is not a food crop, it can

be sprayed with the most toxic chemicals available.

However, a few farmers grow organic cotton, weeding by hand and rotating crops. It is difficult and expensive to grow cotton organically, but doing so dramatically reduces pesticide use on this usually heavily sprayed crop. According to the Sustainable Cotton Project, a California organization working to help cotton growers reduce pesticide use in a low-risk way, cotton cultivation uses approximately 11 percent of the world's pesticides even though it is grown on just 2.4 percent of the world's arable land. Many of these pesticides are carcinogenic (meaning they cause cancer), according to the U.S. Environmental Protection Agency.

Certified organic cotton must be grown in a field that has been pesticide free for at least three years and must be milled on cotton gins that have been completely cleaned of conventional cotton residue. Over the past couple of years, organic cotton production has increased by 53 percent, according to Organic Exchange, a group that is dedicated to organic cotton, and during the next few years, production and sales of this cotton are expected to grow dramatically worldwide.

According to the Sustainable Cotton Project, in California in 2007 there were just two organic cotton farmers growing 240 acres of cotton, which reduced chemical use by a little over 500 pounds. In the same year, there were also twenty-two cotton farmers working to reduce pesticide use, growing 2,000 acres and reducing chemicals by about 2,000 pounds. Their Cleaner Cotton Campaign is a great idea to reduce cotton's negative environmental impact, but when it comes to cotton pet toys, organic is particularly important. We don't chew on our cotton clothes, but our dogs and cats chew on their cotton toys. That means they could be chewing on toxic chemicals.

So when it comes to cotton, go organic! Not only is organic cotton safer for your companion animals, but its production, according to the Organic Trade Association, also replenishes and maintains soil fertility, reduces the use of toxic and persistent pesticides and fertilizers in our environment, and helps to encourage biologically diverse agriculture. Look for dog and cat toys, blankets, beds, and apparel made from this eco-friendly fiber.

Hemp

Talk about hemp and you are likely to get some giggles and wisecracks. "Your cat has a hemp toy? Can I smoke it?" Ha ha, yes, very funny. However, what these wiseacres might not know is that industrial hemp is not the same as the marijuana plant. In fact, it contains so little THC (the psychoactive compound in marijuana) that even if you did smoke it, about all you'd get is a bad headache.

No, hemp's great worth has nothing to do with marijuana, but it does have everything to do with an earth-friendlier approach to manufacturing many of the products we all use every day. Hemp is one of the most environmentally friendly materials ever cultivated by humans.

Hemp bark contains long, soft, strong fibers that are more absorbent and have better insulating qualities than does cotton. This plant is easy to grow organically because very few pests disturb the crops; it also grows quickly and is easily renewed. Hemp produces more pulp per acre than timber does. It can be used to make not only fabric but also paper. Hemp paper manufacturing produces much less wastewater contamination than does conventional paper manufacturing. Hemp production requires very little processing. For example, it doesn't need as many acids for pulping, and its lighter color reduces the need for harsh bleaching.

Hemp paper can be recycled more times than conventional paper can, and hemp also lasts longer than paper does. Archaeologists have found hemp paper that is more than 1,500 years old, and according to *The Columbia History of the World* (Harper and Row, 1984), the oldest relic of human industry is a piece of hemp fabric from 8000 BC!

And if all that weren't enough, the oil of the hemp seed is a great source of essential fatty acids, protein, B vitamins, and fiber. It is used in many dietary supplements for both humans and companion animals.

According to the Hemp Industries Association, in colonial times the law required people to grow hemp. In the eighteenth century, George Washington and Thomas Jefferson grew it. During World War II, the federal government subsidized hemp, in much the same way that it now subsidizes corn and soybeans. During that time, U.S. farmers grew approximately 1 million acres of hemp as part of the subsidy program.

After the war, hemp production largely ceased. The government recognized the difference between industrial hemp and marijuana until the late 1960s, but the passage of the Controlled Substances Act of 1970 blurred those lines, and

ABOUT ALL THOSE Products

Throughout this book, I mention a lot of products. I've been writing about holistic products for many years, and I recommend companies I've talked to and respect as well as products I or my dogs have used and liked. However, one of the most crucial ways to care for the earth is to stop buying so much stuff. Therefore, when I mention products, please know that I am not encouraging you to buy anything that you don't need or that won't be of significant benefit to the animals in your life. At the end of this chapter, see the list of ten criteria to apply before you buy.

hemp production became illegal in the United States.

For many years, the United States had been the only industrialized nation that did not legally permit the production of hemp. Americans could buy, or even make, hemp products, but the hemp had to have originated elsewhere. Hemp farmers and activists are turning that around, state by state. By 2009, twenty-eight states had introduced hemp legislation; fifteen had passed such legislation; and eight had removed barriers to hemp production or research. On April 2, 2009, Representative Ron Paul introduced HR 1866, the Industrial Hemp Farming Act of 2007, with ten original cosponsors, both Democrats and Republicans.

The legislation intends to amend the Controlled Substances Act to exclude industrial hemp from the definition of marijuana, so American farmers can produce eco-friendly hemp and pet-product manufacturers can buy hemp locally. You can follow the news about the legislation at www.votehemp.com/legislation.html.

As the country becomes more open to hemp production, hemp products will likely become more widely available. At present, most hemp products sold in the United States were produced in Canada, where hemp is legally grown, or were produced in the United States out of hemp from Canada or other countries. Look for hemp collars and leashes, beds, apparel, and pet toys.

Bamboo

Bamboo grows quickly, so like hemp, it is an easily renewable natural resource. It does not need any pesticides or fertilizers. That means bamboo products are not only eco-friendly but also safer for pets and people. Bamboo fabric is soft and luxurious as well as strong, and it contains natural properties that kill bacteria and fungus. The material stays cleaner longer and doesn't require hot water for washing. Bamboo fabric absorbs moisture better than cotton does, so it wicks away sweat and odor, making it a great choice for human clothing and for towels. Its chemical-free qualities make it excellent for pet products, too.

Bamboo is a grass that can grow up to four feet in a single day. Bamboo absorbs 45 percent more carbon dioxide from the air than trees do, reduces soil erosion, and doesn't need much water to grow. And don't worry about the pandas. According to Pure Bamboo, a company that makes bamboo products for people, these products aren't made from the same kind of bamboo that pandas eat. Look for collars, harnesses, leashes, and dog apparel of bamboo.

Cork

Durable, impermeable, sound absorbing, and heat insulating, cork is an eco-friendly building material most often used in flooring. It is resistant to many chemicals and holds up well under high traffic, and it costs less than many kinds of hardwood flooring.

Cork is a sustainable crop harvested from the bark of cork oak trees. The bark is harvested without harming the tree and regrows about every nine years, much more quickly than it takes to regrow other trees. Although cork isn't a common material for pet products (yet), I have seen dog collars made of cork.

Rain Forest Botanicals

We all know the rain forest is at risk. You've probably heard that you should avoid buying products contributing to the destruction of the rain forests. However, products made from renewable rain forest botanicals encourage preservation of one of our earth's most valuable natural resources. Producing these products also helps support indigenous cultures. Holistic health practitioners sometimes use or recommend rain forest

Sustainable Pet Paraphernalia

Is that toy, dog bed, or collar sustainable?
Check the materials against this chart:

SUSTAINABLE	WHERE YOU MIGHT FIND IT
Bamboo	Building materials, collars and harnesses, dog apparel, leashes
Cork	Dog collars and flooring
Hemp	Dog and cat collars, leashes, beds, apparel, and toys, including rope toys
Organic cotton	Dog and cat apparel, blankets, beds, toys
Rain forest products	Some pet supplements are made with rain forest herbs
Recycled material (such as soda bottles or recycled fabric remnants)	Collars, dog beds, leashes, and toys

botanicals for pets to aid in digestion and to help heal skin problems. Some rain forest herbs help calm stressed-out, anxious animals, and some are used in grooming products.

Simple

The bottom line when it comes to consumerism is that living more simply is better for the earth. Buying less means generating less trash, using less fuel, and squandering fewer resources. And living more simply? That means you have more time and less mental clutter, so you can enjoy the simple pleasures of life more—things like taking your dog for a walk and breathing in the fresh air, taking in the view, just *being* in nature, or reading a book with a purring cat on your lap. Cats are warm. You can turn down your heat.

Ten Earth-Friendly Buying Criteria

Sometimes you do need to buy things. The question is, what are you going to buy? How are you going to vote with your dollars? What message do you want to send to corporate America?

Pick up that product. Take a good hard look at it. Be critical. Ask questions. Carefully examine the contents as well as the packaging. Call the company, and ask questions about where the materials were sourced. Does the company have other "green" practices? Let the company sell you on its products.

If your companion animal really needs it or can truly benefit from it, and you can afford it, and the following ten criteria (or at least most of them) apply, then you've probably got yourself a good buy.

Is it durable? Well made? Does it look like it will last, as opposed to being disposable or cheaply put together?

When it is no longer usable, can it be recycled? Can the packaging be recycled?

Is it made from recycled ingredients/materials? Is the packaging made from recycled materials?

Does it reveal the sources of its ingredients/materials? If you call the company and ask about sources, do you feel like the person you are talking to is being straight with you?

Is it produced sustainably? Is it made from renewable resources, such as hemp, organic cotton, bamboo, cork, or rain forest–friendly products?

If it goes into a pet's mouth (food, treats, toys), is it organic, or does it contain all-natural ingredients? Are you sure?

Is the manufacturing process earth friendly or earth friendlier than processes for similar products? Does the manufacturer use wind power or solar power? Electric rather than gas?

Is it local or regional? Did it have to travel less than halfway across the country to get to you?

Is it cruelty free? Did animals die to make it? Did people suffer to make it? Were human rights and animal welfare considered?

Does the company contribute to any charitable organizations or participate in any other activities that give back to the earth or animal causes?

Over the years, I've come across a lot of pet product companies. I've interviewed many of them and asked them about what they are doing to make the world a better place. Some of them have great answers. Others? Not so great. In the Resources section of this book, you will find a list of the companies that have impressed me over the years. These companies sell collars, leashes, beds, apparel, and lots of other eco-friendly pet products, including food, treats, and supplements. If you really decide you do need to buy something for your pet and you're not sure where to find it, I recommend those companies.

Chapter 5

Healthy
Animals,
Healthy Earth

Holistic =

Earth Friendly

Each living being on the earth is like a microcosm of the planet itself. The earth constitutes a giant, complex ecosystem, and all of its parts work together. A network of streams, rivers, and oceans flow through it. It has layers of rock, soil, and plant life under layers of air and stratosphere. Living things populate it.

Each body on the earth is similarly its own complex ecosystem, with networks of blood vessels and passageways for oxygen, food, and waste. The body has layers of bone, muscle, and skin and is populated with microscopic organisms. Some help (such as beneficial bacteria that aid in our digestion); some hurt (such as viruses that make us sick).

To heal our planet, we have to step back and see where we are helping and where we are hurting. In the same way, holistic health is a whole-body approach that steps back and examines every piece to discover which parts are out of balance. Is your companion animal getting too much food, too little exercise, too much chemical exposure, not enough attention? Is your

Green Guidance

Because *holistic* is trendy right now but not a legally defined term, anyone can use it to describe anything. Don't just buy a product because it is labeled holistic. Find out whether it is something that will benefit your companion animal. Apply the Ten Earth-Friendly Buying Criteria (see pages 68-69) to any product, no matter how "green" or "natural" the label looks. Along those same lines, be as choosy about a holistic health practitioner as you would be about a regular veterinarian. Any holistic health practitioner should have extensive training, be reputable in the field, and have references.

companion animal's body an environment that promotes the spread of a virus or an environment that promotes a strong immune system?

In other words, a holistic approach to health is an earth-friendly approach. Not only is a look at the big picture a more natural way to promote health and heal the body, but it also encourages more natural healing techniques, ones that don't load the body with chemicals or just treat symptoms in isolation without examining the reason why they might have emerged in the first place.

Holistic health is trendy in the pet industry right now; in fact, it's big business. That means a lot of companies have figured out that if they put words such as *holistic* and *natural* and *eco-friendly* on their packaging, they are more likely to sell their merchandise. Buying every such product you see in the name of saving the earth and doing the best for your

Green Words

Thousands upon thousands of persons have studied disease. Almost no one has studied health.

—Adelle Davis,
American nutritionist and author

companion animals is not exactly in keeping with living more simply and consuming less—values that have a significant impact on the earth.

However, the principle behind holistic health is definitely earth friendly. So how do you live in harmony with the earth and give your companion animals all the benefits of a holistic approach to health and wellness without spending all your hard-earned cash? This chapter will help you sort out how to approach health holistically in a sensible, simple, earth-friendly way, without generating a lot of extra trash or going broke or funneling all your money to people who probably won't actually help you or your pet.

What Is Holistic/ Complementary Health Care?

First, let's define a few terms. *Holistic* is an adjective that comes from the word *whole*, and it is used to describe an approach to health that looks at the entire person or animal, rather than at an isolated disease or symptom. For example, if your Labrador Retriever has itchy skin or a hot spot (an oozy, itchy, infected area), a holistic veterinarian will look at the skin—but not just the skin. He might ask what your Lab has been eating, how much he is sleeping,

how he is acting, how *you* are acting. Have you changed his diet? Is he getting enough exercise and attention? Have you started cleaning your carpets with a new chemical or washed his bedding with a new detergent? Is there a new stressor in the home, such as a move or a new pet? Are *you* stressed out? Animals tend to mirror our feelings, and one of the most common reasons for companion animal stress is stress in the humans living in the household.

In other words, every aspect of your companion animal's life, from a holistic point of view, can have an impact on every other aspect. Disease isn't isolated. It is the result of an imbalance within the entire system, so to correct the disease, the holistic healer tries to balance the system. Once balanced and unpolluted, the body (like the earth) is fairly good at fixing its own problems.

Sometimes, however, conventional medicine is appropriate. If your companion animal breaks a bone, gets hit by a car, ruptures a spinal disk, or has a sudden acute illness or infection, modern conventional veterinary care is very good at fixing these serious problems quickly. Veterinary sciences have progressed far beyond anything most people could have imagined just a decade ago. We now have the technology to deal with many serious

illnesses that used to be a death sentence for companion animals. In many cases, your conventional veterinarian really does know the best course of treatment, especially now that an increasing number of veterinarians are practicing a complementary

Green Guidance

Vaccinations sound preventive, and they are—in a way. However, many companion animals suffer serious reactions to vaccinations, and many veterinarians believe pets are overvaccinated. Some even think that other health problems, such as cancer, might be related to vaccinations. All new puppies and kittens should have their initial sets of vaccinations, as recommended by your veterinarian, to guard against life-threatening diseases when they are most vulnerable, as well as to keep these diseases out of the general animal population. Distemper used to be a leading cause of death in pet dogs. Today, it's rare because of vaccinations. Some vaccinations are required by law, such as the rabies vaccine, but don't automatically assume that you need to visit the veterinarian for those annual booster shots throughout your companion animal's adult life. More vets are now altering vaccination schedules to vaccinate less often because of concerns about the risks. Talk to your veterinarian about how often your animals really require vaccination, so you can come up with a vaccination schedule everyone can feel good about.

Green Words

Holistic (or integrative or complementary) veterinary medicine is the examination and diagnosis of an animal, considering all aspects of the animal's life and employing all of the practitioner's senses, as well as the combination of conventional and alternative (or complementary) modalities of treatment. When a holistic veterinarian sees a pet, besides giving it a comprehensive physical examination, he/she wants to find out all about its behaviors, distant medical and dietary history, and its environment including diet, emotional stresses, and other factors. Holistic medicine, by its very nature, is humane to the core. The wholeness of its scope will set up a lifestyle for the animal that is most appropriate. The techniques used in holistic medicine are gentle, minimally invasive, and incorporate patient well-being and stress reduction. Holistic thinking is centered on love, empathy and respect.

—American Holistic Veterinary Medical Association, www.ahvma.org

approach, employing both conventional and holistic viewpoints.

Complementary health care utilizes the best of both worlds, combining conventional veterinary medicine with more natural and holistic approaches, as each is appropriate. It's easy to fall into the trap of believing that one or the other type of health care is all good or all bad, but that's simply not true. Conventional medicine is sometimes exactly what an animal needs, and the training conventional veterinarians receive is appropriate for many situations.

At other times, holistic approaches will be exactly what an animal needs. These methods don't always agree: for example, holistic approaches tend to avoid pharmaceutical medicine in favor of slower-acting but more natural remedies, such as herbs and lifestyle changes; the conventional approach is more likely to involve a prescription. But with a little common sense, they can mean the ultimate in holistic care for your companion animal—a big-picture view that embraces all of the possible approaches to health and wellness. (If only more people looked at the world in that way.)

Prevention: The Key to a Holistic Approach

While conventional medicine tends to treat diseases, holistic health care focuses on prevention. That's not to say conventional care doesn't make prevention a priority, however. When your veterinarian advises well-pet visits every year, part of those visits are about prevention—keeping your animal healthy and catching any problems before they get too advanced.

Of course, sometimes even the healthiest and most well-adjusted animals (and people) get sick, even with preventive care. We can't always know why. But, to minimize the chances of illness, approach life holistically. Look at the big picture, and keep the whole system in balance. It's the part of your companion animal's health that you can control.

To practice preventive care, cover the basics below.

🔥 Feed a high-quality, nutritionally complete diet. Don't feed too much food or too many treats. Keep your companion animal at a healthy weight.

🔥 Provide a chance to exercise at least once every day and an opportunity to enjoy fresh air and sunlight on most days.

🔥 Provide plenty of opportunities for mental stimulation, such as training sessions, traveling to new places and meeting new people, and doing challenging activities such as running obstacle courses or playing games.

🔥 Spend time with your companion animal every day. Let your animals *be* companions. Include them in family activities.

🔥 Touch your cat, dog, rabbit, small animal, or bird. Pet them with affection and kindness. They like that. Both humans and animals benefit from touch. Why do you think they are called "pets"?

💧 Groom your companion animal regularly: bathe, trim nails, and brush teeth.

💧 Practice stress management. When you are stressed, your companion animals feel it, too.

💧 Visit the veterinarian for an annual checkup, but do not overvaccinate.

If your animal does experience a health problem, consider alternative treatments as well as responsible conventional care. Could a gentle herbal, homeopathic, or flower remedy help? What about acupuncture, a visit to the veterinary chiropractor, or a massage?

Consider visiting a holistic veterinarian, especially one who embraces a complementary approach. Find one through the American Holistic Veterinary Medical Association at www.ahvma.org. Click on "Find a Holistic Vet."

Guide to Holistic Therapies

Many holistic therapies benefit companion animals not experiencing any health problems; they are also great for those trying to overcome an imbalance of some sort. This imbalance may take the form of a disease or chronic condition, from minor issues such as creaky joints, itchy skin, and low energy to more serious problems such as diabetes, hip dysplasia, bladder stones, glaucoma, and cancer. Following are brief descriptions of some of the more common holistic/complementary approaches being applied to companion animals today. Check them out, and consider integrating the ones that interest you into your companion animal's life—and maybe your own life, too.

Nutritional Therapy

When tainted commercial pet food poisoned thousands of animals in 2007, the average consumer suddenly became more aware of what might be in lurking inside a bag of kibble. However, that wasn't the beginning of nutritional therapy. Long before the tragic pet food scandal, holistically oriented vets and even pet food manufacturers advised improving a pet's diet to improve a pet's health.

Cheap dog food contains a lot of artificial ingredients and fillers—the equivalent of a diet of cheap fast food for humans. Some dogs get by on these foods, but others develop many food-related health problems, from skin allergies to gastrointestinal problems to (some researchers believe) cancer.

Many holistic health practitioners say that the first step any pet owner should take to improve a pet's health is to feed a better diet, as a pet's diet is extremely important for overall health. In fact, no matter what health issue your companion animals are having, a high-quality diet will support healing whether that includes dog food made of high-quality natural ingredients, a home-cooked diet, a carefully formulated diet of raw food, or a combination.

Holistic veterinarians practicing nutritional therapy will make dietary prescriptions to improve or maximize health and may also test for food allergies and sensitivities in order to discover the source of the health problems.

Doga

And you thought yoga was just for you? Doga is a new trend in yoga classes that includes both people and their dogs. Dogs do yoga naturally—when they stretch after getting up postnap, they almost always do both the upward facing dog and downward facing dog poses (which were named after those exact movements)—but you may never have considered including your dog in your own practice. Dog classes are offered in many big cities, from San Francisco, California, to Jacksonville Beach, Florida, and even in Canada and Japan. You help your dog into position and incorporate him into your own poses, so you really are doing yoga together. Dogs also get to enjoy pet massage during class. Ask local yoga teachers or dog trainers whether there are doga classes available in your area, or look for yoga teacher Suzi Teitelman's Doga DVD, soon to be released, to try it at home.

Supplements

Conventional wisdom says that a high-quality dog food is all the nutrition your dog needs, but that wisdom is giving way to the notion that individually tweaking an animal's system with the right remedies might maximize health and even cure disease. Manufacturers of animal supplements cannot *say* they are to be used to treat or cure any disease—that's the law. However, a holistic veterinarian may be able to give you some more frank advice about what supplementation can and cannot do for your animal.

There are many kinds of supplements, and within each category there exists a wide range of qualities. Currently, the government doesn't regulate animal supplements. They fall into a gray area between being a food and a drug, so state regulators aren't sure what to do about them and tend to handle them differently from one state to another. To address this problem, the industry has developed some self-policing strategies to help guard against less ethical manufacturers whose supplements don't contain the ingredients they claim or don't contain enough of an ingredient to actually make a difference. These strategies include voluntary quality-control assurance programs and membership in trade organizations with high standards, such as the National Animal Supplement Council (NASC) (http://nasc.cc).

The main kinds of supplements available for animals today are listed below.

Dietary supplements/nutraceuticals: These supplements could fill in any nutritional gaps in your dog's food. Some include live enzymes and probiotics that your pet would get if he ate raw food in the wild, to make up for what processed kibble lacks. Some include ingredients

such as glucosamine, for stronger and more flexible joints, or essential fatty acids, for healthier skin and coat. Your holistic veterinarian can recommend appropriate supplements for your companion animal's individual needs. Some knowledgeable retail pet store owners specializing in holistic products may also be able to make recommendations for you.

Herbal supplements and Chinese herbs: Usually gentler and slower acting than chemical pharmaceuticals, herbal remedies may help resolve many medical problems in pets and support healthy functioning of organ systems. These remedies may come in pills, powders, or liquids and may be made of individual herbs (such as valerian or chamomile, for calming) or combinations of herbs (such as ginger, mint, and fennel, for upset stomachs). A qualified herbalist or holistic veterinarian can advise you about which herbs would be appropriate for your companion animal. For more information about herbal remedies, I like the book *Herbs for Pets*, by Gregory L. Tilford and Mary L. Wulff.

Homeopathic remedies: Homeopathy is a method for balancing the body's health through the concept of "like cures like." Substances known to cause symptoms in large doses are drastically diluted into harmless remedies that spark a healing

reaction in a body experiencing those same symptoms. Although homeopathy sounds counterintuitive, plenty of people believe it works and have experiences to back up their claims. To learn more about homeopathy or to find a homeopathic veterinarian, visit the Academy of Veterinary Homeopathy at www.theavh.org.

Flower essences: Flower essences are waters that have been infused with the vibrations of different flowers. They are for healing on an energetic rather than physical level, and many people swear these essences help balance emotionally distraught or stressed-out pets. Rescue Remedy is one of the most popular flower essences for stress reduction. You can give it to your anxious pets during a thunderstorm or even take it yourself. In fact, many flower essence practitioners recommend always taking the same essences that you give your animal, since their emotional distresses probably mirror your own. To learn more about flower essences, visit the Web page of the Flower Essence Society at www.flowersociety.org.

Pet Physical Therapies

Holistic veterinarians and other health practitioners use many of the same physical therapies on pets that humans have been using for years. These therapies manipulate the physical body or the energetic body to balance the system, so the body can heal itself.

Acupuncture: Used to treat everything from joint pain to kidney failure, acupuncture has many fans. People say it decreases pain and other uncomfortable symptoms in pets, even though Western researchers don't really know why it works. This ancient practice involves inserting ultrathin needles into certain parts of the body. Surprisingly, most pets don't seem to mind. For more information and to find a veterinary acupuncturist, see the American Academy of Veterinary Acupuncture Web site at www.aava.org.

Chiropractic care: Many people swear by their chiropractor, and an increasing number also claim great benefits for their pets after visiting a veterinary chiropractor, who manipulates the body to realign it for better health and healing. To find a veterinary chiropractor, see the American Veterinary Chiropractic Association Web site at www.animalchiropractic.org.

Pet massage: Many pets truly enjoy a good massage, and you can give your companion animal a massage at home. However, if your companion animal has an orthopedic problem, regular massages by a professional pet massage therapist, using any of several massage and bodywork methods (including energy work such as Reiki, which manipulates a pet's energy field rather than physical body), might reduce pain and increase mobility. To find an animal massage therapist near you, visit the International Association of Animal Massage and Bodywork Web site at www.iaamb.org. Some animal massage therapists also do chiropractic adjustments or energy healing or both. Be sure the therapist you choose is well trained.

When it comes to health care, the eco-friendly way really is better for our companion animals and our planet, but sometimes less is also more. So step back, look at the *holistic* picture, and choose the right care when appropriate, according to your comfort level. Holistic methods aren't for everyone, but any pet owner can probably get on board with preventing health problems through an approach to the whole animal.

As our culture continues to evolve, holistic health options are getting more and more popular every day, so if you choose them for yourself, consider them for your animal. Mother nature's big-picture wisdom and natural healing resources can help puppies and kittens grow up healthier and seniors age more gracefully, and they can help *you* feel better, too.

Chapter 6

Green
Begins at Home

A Kinder,
Gentler,
Greener,
Safer Home

You know what they say: pollution begins at home. Wait, maybe that's not what they say! At least, that's not how things should be. However, because we are such a chemically dependent society, our homes have become filled with toxins that can compromise our health as well as the health of our companion animals.

Some of those toxins are particularly hazardous to our pets, from the leaking antifreeze on the garage floor to the fumes that are released by carpeting and the chemicals that are used in household cleaning products.

Our animals live much closer to the ground than we do. They roll on the floor, sleep on the floor, and eat off the floor.

Inside the house, their bare paws and skin are exposed to cleaning product residue and fumes, while outside, they can be exposed to harsh deicing salts, toxic mulch in the garden, and lawn chemicals. In fact, domesticated animals have a much higher chemical exposure than animals in the wild do, even if wild animals occasionally nibble on pesticide-laden crops.

Green Words

And if your animals are exposed to all those chemicals, what about your kids? What about *you*?

A big part of the environmental movement today concerns purifying our personal living spaces, which are (like our bodies) microcosms of the planet. Greening your home exemplifies thinking globally but acting locally. Not only will you reduce your own family's toxic exposure, but you also will be setting an example for others who might not otherwise think to reduce their own carbon footprints at home.

Once again, you'll be voting with your dollars by purchasing eco-friendly products over toxic ones. You might even help to prevent future disease, from chronic allergies to cancer, in your companion animals and your human family members. Isn't that worth the effort of cleaning up your act?

Cleaning Up Your Act

Cleaning is a little bit of an environmental conundrum.

We don't want our homes to be dirty and full of germs, and we need to clean up the toxins and pollutants that people and pets track in from the outside world. However, we don't want to douse our living environments in cleaning chemicals, either.

Cleaning chemicals can be hazardous for the health of our pets (especially for dogs and cats with sensitive skin and allergies), not to mention our children and even adults with chemical sensitivities. Fumes

from chemical cleaners can be hazardous to lung tissue, and direct contact with carpet and furniture cleaning chemicals can cause serious skin reactions in any living creature with sensitive skin. Birds and small animals are also particularly vulnerable to chemical exposure.

For safety's sake, we need to keep our homes both cleaner and safer.

But who says you have to clean with all those chemicals? A century ago, most cleaning was probably accomplished with good old-fashioned soap and water. Cleaning up your home safely isn't actually that hard, and it will be easier on your budget, too. Just follow the eight rules listed below for a greener, cleaner, safer home.

DON'T assume you need to use a cleaner. Sometimes, plain old water is a perfectly effective cleanser. For tougher jobs, a little eco-friendly soap (such as castile soap) and water or a little baking soda and white vinegar may be all the cleaner you require. If you get used to cleaning without cleaning products, you will not only lighten the chemical load in your home but also save money.

DON'T use any cleaning product that has the words *danger, warning,* or *caution* on the label. These products are potentially fatal to pets and children, and you can certainly clean your house without them.

DON'T use a product containing any of the following ingredients, which can be highly toxic to humans, pets, and/or the environment: ammonia (common in all-purpose cleaners and glass cleaner), chlorine bleach (common in cleaning products), lye or acid (in drain, oven, and

toilet bowl cleaners), naphtha (a petroleum-distilled product common in cleaning products and solvents), phosphates (common in laundry detergents), solvents (common in stain removers and all-purpose cleaners), synthetic dye (common in cleaning products), synthetic fragrance (common in cleaning products), and any chemical name you don't recognize.

DON'T ever clean your floors and carpets with toxic chemicals. Your companion animals are *down there.* If you have young children, they are down there, too. Floor cleaners often contain dangerous solvents made with petrochemicals. They aren't just harmful for pets and kids right after you use them. They build up in our homes over time to produce an even more toxic effect. They also contaminate the environment when washed down the drain. Use plant-based, nontoxic floor cleaners instead.

DO read the label on cleaning products. Even if it is called "Eco-Clean" or something else that implies it is eco-friendly, that may only mean that it has taken some toxic elements out of its original formula. It may still have others.

DO look for ingredients you recognize to be safe. The safest, least toxic cleaners

Greener Cleaner

You will need the following ingredients to make a greener cleaner:

- 1 cup hot water
- 1 teaspoon baking soda
- 1 cup flat club soda
- 1 teaspoon liquid castile soap (find it in your local drugstore or natural foods store)
- ¼ teaspoon tea tree oil (find it in your local drugstore or natural foods store)

Combine the hot water and baking soda in a 4-cup glass measure or a bowl, and stir until the baking soda dissolves. Stir in the club soda, castile soap, and tea tree oil. Pour into a spray bottle. Spray on surfaces, and let it stand a few minutes, then scrub clean.

after each use, quickly sweep and damp-mop floors every day or two, and vacuum frequently, you will rarely if ever need to use heavy-duty cleaning products, making it much less tempting to bring more toxic chemicals into your home.

DO make a batch of the simple all-purpose cleaner shown in the box "Greener Cleaner" to use on all the surfaces you would normally spray with a cleaner, especially in the kitchen and bathroom. This cleaner releases no dangerous fumes and won't hurt pets. The alkaline minerals in the baking soda and the club soda dissolve dirt and odor, and the tea tree oil lends this cleaner natural antibacterial properties.

Garage Safety

The garage is home to some of a typical household's most hazardous chemicals. In particular, antifreeze contains ethylene glycol, which is extremely toxic and potentially fatal if dogs or cats ingest even a small amount. Antifreeze poisoning probably kills thousands of companion animals and wild animals every year because, unfortunately, antifreeze smells and tastes sweet. It is poisonous for humans, too—just two tablespoons can seriously harm a child.

Even if you keep your garage floor clean and your car leak free, why would you want to have such a toxic chemical in your garage? Fortunately, there are alternatives to antifreeze with ethylene glycol. Brands made with propylene glycol are just as safe for your car but less toxic to people, pets, and wildlife. Look for Sierra antifreeze/coolant: www.sierraantifreeze.com, (800) 323-5440. (Note: Many processed

are made primarily from plant-based products such as plant oils, rather than synthetic chemicals.

DO clean often. The more you clean, the less difficult the job will be. Light cleaning requires fewer and less concentrated products. If you swish the toilet with a brush every morning, wipe down the sinks and tub foods contain small amounts of propylene glycol. This chemical might be fine for safer antifreeze but for food? Yuck. Just one more good reason to read labels.)

Make sure no other fluids from your car have leaked out on to your garage floor or driveway, and, if they do, clean them up immediately. It's worth checking daily, just to be sure. Make sure as well that any hazardous cleaning, maintenance, and lawn chemicals are out of reach of children and animals. Better yet, dispose of them all safely (see chapter 8) and replace items, as you need them, with organic and nontoxic alternatives.

Another winter-weather hazard: deicing chemicals. Salt-based chemicals that melt ice can be hazardous to children and pets, irritate paw pads, kill your plants and lawns, and even leach into the drinking water. Of course, a slippery walk is treacherous, too.

Instead of a salt-based product, try sprinkling sand on ice to create a nonslip surface. Or use a salt-free eco-friendlier deicing product such as Safe Paw (www.safepaw.com), which you can find at pet stores and hardware stores.

Breathe Easier

Indoor air quality might not be the first thing that comes to mind when you are thinking about cleaning up your home, but air quality can have a big impact on the health of anyone in your home. You cannot see a lot of the air pollutants in your home, but they are having their effect, most ominously in the form of volatile organic compounds (VOCs). These are gases released into the air that can damage eye, nose, throat, and lung tissue. They have been linked to liver and kidney damage and even cancer, not to mention to allergies, respiratory problems, and chronic headaches.

VOCs are released by building materials, carpets, paint, treated wood, furniture, office supplies, cleaning products, cosmetics, air fresheners, dry-cleaned clothes, pesticides and other lawn and garden chemicals, and even craft supplies. To clean up the air in your home, you can:

🍃 Use eco-friendly building materials that don't contain VOCs for all future home improvement projects.

🍃 Only buy zero-VOC paint and other finishers.

🍃 Never use pressure-treated wood or particle board in your home.

Green Guidance

If you suspect your dog or cat has ingested even a little bit of antifreeze, go to the veterinarian right away. When treated immediately, animals can sometimes be saved. Treatment usually includes inducing vomiting and administering activated charcoal, which absorbs the ethylene glycol. The animal may also need intravenous ethyl alcohol to counteract the effects of the ethylene glycol.

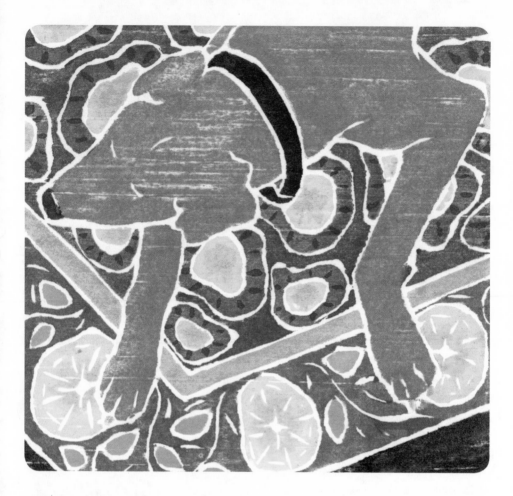

Do not use synthetic carpet, which emits large amounts of VOCs. Look for natural flooring options instead, such as natural fiber carpet, tile, stone, hardwood, bamboo, and cork.

Don't use any cleaning products

Green Guidance

Every time you need to add something new to your home, such as furniture, appliances, carpet, or flooring, consider nontoxic, environmentally friendly products. Building materials such as stone, tile, bamboo, cork, and natural fiber carpeting and furniture don't deplete the planet's resources and don't release toxic fumes into your home, keeping everybody in your family safer, including the most sensitive members, children and animals.

with VOCs. Look for nontoxic, botanical-based cleaners instead.

🔥 Don't use PVC products such as plastic shower curtains. Try a cloth shower curtain instead.

🔥 Buy organic bedding, including sheets (which may be treated with formaldehyde!), mattresses, and pillows made without synthetic foam.

🔥 Don't use aerosol products.

🔥 Fill your home with plants, which absorb some VOCs from the air.

Consider using air purifiers with charcoal filters in your home; they can reduce your exposure to VOCs. Put them in rooms mostly likely to contain VOCs, such as those with new carpeting or those containing office equipment, and rooms where you spend a lot of time.

The Garbage Situation

Each person in America generates, on average, 4.4 pounds of garbage every single day. In a year, that adds up to about 1,600 pounds of garbage per person. This garbage not only fills up landfills and generates methane (a greenhouse gas) but also is a by-product of our obsession with acquiring stuff. Garbage can also be directly hazardous to our companion animals, who often like to check it out to see if it contains anything good to eat or fun to play with. According to pet insurance companies, poisoning is one of the most common threats to the health of dogs and cats in the home, and a lot of that poisoning comes from garbage.

Your companion animals can become very sick (or worse) or can suffer intestinal

Green Guidance

What's so bad about weeds? Sure, crabgrass isn't exactly attractive, but some weeds actually benefit your lawn and the earth. For example, according to an article about lawn care on Grinning Planet (www.grinningplanet .com, a Web site that takes a fun and humorous approach to environmental issues), clover infuses your lawn with more nitrogen, makes your lawn look greener, provides nectar for bees, encourages earthworms, resists disease, and is drought tolerant, and you can even eat the flowers, which contain protein, calcium, phosphorus, and magnesium. Try tossing them in your salad (but only if they haven't been sprayed with lawn chemicals!).

blockages or choking by getting into the trash and swallowing spoiled food, discarded medication, bones, coffee grounds, tea bags, and human foods that may be toxic to them, such as onions, grapes, raisins, and chocolate. Animals can also be poisoned by chewing on the containers of

toxic products, such as cleaning solutions and insecticides.

The best way to protect your companion animals from the hazards of your garbage is to make certain that garbage is always safely secured so pets can't get into it. Another great solution is to produce less garbage, and make the garbage you do generate less toxic. Some ways to do this include the following:

Not buying toxic cleaning products. Use natural, safe products with biodegradable packaging instead (see the previous section).

Putting coffee, tea, and producing scraps/leftovers into a compost bucket and mix them into your garden rather than throwing them away. Coffee grounds, tea bags, and leftover coffee and unsweetened tea also make great plant food for your houseplants. (Just be sure your pets can't get into the plants.)

Going vegetarian. You won't generate any dangerous bones or fatty, spoiled meat scraps.

For more information about disposing of your garbage in an environmentally conscious way, see chapter 8.

Your Lawn and Garden

Some of the worst toxic chemicals home owners use go on the grass and the garden—the very places our pets like to play, roll on, and dig. A chemically treated lawn is dangerous for pets and people, especially kids. Studies have linked lawn chemicals to health issues, including cancer, in both children and companion animals.

If you have your lawn professionally treated, look into nontoxic options. More lawn care and landscaping companies are offering nontoxic or organic choices. Or consider caring for your lawn organically yourself. You and your pets can spend more time together outside.

According to the informative Web site SafeLawns.org (www.safelawns.org), not only are organic lawn care products safer for animals and humans, but they also actually improve soil quality and strengthen the grass, making your lawn healthier and more beautiful. Just as a healthy diet balances and strengthens your immune system, a natural, organic "diet" for your lawn brings it into balance, so it resists pests and environmental stressors with more vigor. You'll end up having to water and mow less often, and that translates into more free time. In addition, the energy, chemical load, and pollution from mowing, watering, and fertilizing lawns across the United States make up 2 percent of our country's total fossil fuel consumption and 10 percent of air pollution, according to SafeLawns.org.

More and more companies are making organic fertilizers, weed killers, pesticides, and soil amendment products. Some lawn care companies also offer organic care options. Ask your local garden store, or check out the resource directory on the Web site www.safelawns.org.

If you don't already have one, consider purchasing a mulching mower. These mowers automatically recycle grass clippings, delivering them back into the lawn where they belong. Grass clippings contain nitrogen, so they are a natural fertilizer. When they decompose, that nitrogen goes right back into the soil so your lawn can use it again. Grass mulch can also discourage weed growth in the lawn. According to studies at the University of Connecticut, lawns with clippings left on them had 45 percent less crabgrass, 45 percent more earthworms, 25 percent greater root mass, and 60 percent more water reaching the plant roots, compared with lawns without clippings. A mulching mower can completely eliminate your need for lawn chemicals. Doesn't that make it seem kind of ridiculous to spend all that time raking, bagging, and disposing of your lawn clippings in a landfill?

Below are a few more natural lawn care tips to keep your backyard pet friendly.

Choose native grass. Grass native to your area will grow better because it will be adapted to your local temperatures and rainfall levels.

Don't stop using your mulching mower when the leaves fall. Mow over leaves instead of raking them. This breaks down the leaves, which then naturally enrich the soil before winter hits.

Mow less often. Not only will you use less fuel and generate less pollution, but taller grass grows more slowly, looks lusher, and delivers more nutrients to the root system, so the lawn grows stronger and resists drought better. That means less watering and less damage from exuberant pets' running back and forth after tennis balls.

Test the pH of your soil. If your soil is naturally acidic (you can buy a pH soil test at your garden store), add wood ashes from your fireplace in the fall and again in the spring to help alkalinize the soil for better lawn growth and stifled weed growth.

Aerate your lawn with an aeration machine. You'll nourish the soil and root system naturally, without having to resort to chemicals.

Lawn chemicals aren't the only toxins that could potentially harm your companion animals. To be eco-friendlier and safer, too, avoid using the products listed here.

Pest poisons: If you have to get rid of moles, gophers, slugs, or any other pests, there are many nontoxic mechanical methods (like live traps, physical barriers, or picking off bugs and squashing them) and nontoxic homemade remedies that you can mix up and spray on plants. For more about organic gardening, check out Organic Gardening's online magazine at www.organicgardening.com. They will keep you up to date on the very latest trends in organic gardening.

Insect-repelling candles and torches: "Citronella" sounds pretty natural, but if animals ingest it, they can suffer from severe gastrointestinal symptoms like vomiting and diarrhea.

Cocoa bean mulch: This mulch also sounds natural, and it is a nice (and fragrant) ornamental mulch for landscaping, but unfortunately, chocolate is toxic to most companion animals and ingesting this mulch could harm them. Instead, consider using decorative gravel or wood mulch. For mulch to amend soil, consider grass clippings, leaf mold, or compost.

As for you gardeners, are you still spraying with pesticides? Dousing with fertilizers? On a quest for the perfect unblemished pest-free produce? It's the twenty-first century, and organic gardening has become a popular hobby, so consider switching your methods. You'll grow safer food for your family and help to maintain a safer outdoor space for your pets. It's easier than ever before to grow your own vegetables and flowers without toxic chemicals. Bookstores, magazine racks, and the Internet boast organic gardening resources brimming with information on how to deter pests, enrich soil, and grow big, beautiful produce without harsh chemicals.

The safer, cleaner, and greener your house and yard, the more at home you will feel. Make your home a haven against a world that is filled with pollution and chemicals, and you, your children, and your companion animals will all breathe a little bit easier.

Green Tip

Wouldn't your cat love it if you planted a patch of catnip in your herb garden? Catnip is a hardy member of the mint family and grows easily without chemical encouragement—maybe too easily. If you do decide to sow catnip seeds, allow plenty of space. Catnip plants tend to take over the garden.

Chapter 7

Get
Involved

The Many

Faces of

Activism

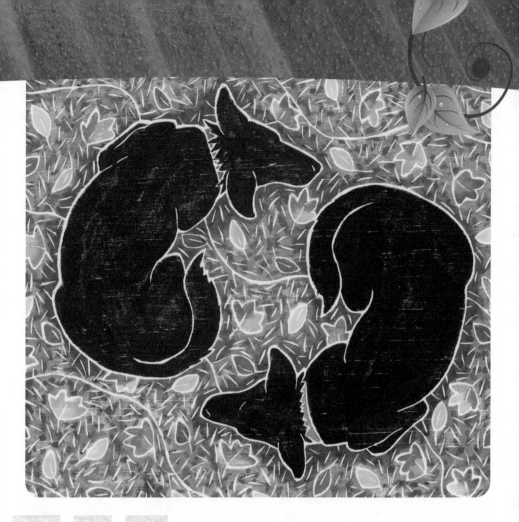

We live in an imperfect world, and we can just accept that fact and live with it, or we can try to change it with purpose and intention. The people who try to change the world through action are activists. The word *activist* has a negative connotation in many circles, I think

because it is often associated with the word *extremist*, someone so narrowly devoted to a single view that he or she cannot see the big picture. Although every cause has its extremists, this label is pretty unfair. Activism has many faces. It is activism to write a letter to your editor, to choose not to support factory farming, to ride your bicycle instead of drive your car. It is activism to

carry a sign at a protest or just to show up at a protest and be part of the crowd. It is activism to adopt a companion animal from a shelter or be a foster home for a rescue group. It is activism to curb your consumerism, your processed food consumption, or your trash production.

At its heart, activism is simply *acting* on your beliefs. You don't have to get violent or

> We all are responsible for the sins of our society. We are all involved either through omission or commission.
>
> —Rabbi Marshall T. Meyer,
> international human rights activist

illegal or even unreasonable about it. Yes, some activists are all these things. Some are also incredibly passionate and know how to make change happen. Others just want to help a little or ease into a cause rather than jumping in with both feet.

The world has plenty of room for all these types, and as we evolve toward a cleaner, gentler, more caring, and more enlightened society, anyone who wants to make a difference can do it in a way that works for him or her. There are many ways to make a difference. All you have to do is have the desire.

Anybody reading this book probably believes fairly strongly in a few things, including making the earth a better and cleaner place, preserving our natural resources for future generations, and of course keeping our companion animals a safe, healthy, and happy part of our lives. If you are recycling, if you adopted your companion animals from the local shelter, if you buy local food or grow an organic garden, you are already making a difference. But maybe you want to do more.

Getting involved in a cause close to your heart can be incredibly gratifying and fulfilling because you are being proactive and actually living your beliefs. That shows integrity, especially when you know you

will have to deal with people who don't share or understand your views. But you also have to know how to get involved in a way that makes sense for your life and fits your personality. Are you the type to drop it all and go join Greenpeace, or are you more the type to volunteer to walk the dogs at your local shelter? Knowing how to get involved in the cause that means the most to you is the next step, and that's where this chapter comes in. First, you have to clarify your priorities, then you have to figure out the best way to act.

What Are You For and What Are You Against?

The first step to making a real difference in the world is clarifying what you believe and what your priorities are. You may see many wrongs you would like to make right, but to avoid burnout, it's crucial to have positive achievable goals as well. For instance, being *against* global warming is important but that stance, in and of itself, is not positive. Being *for* honoring the earth and appreciating it by spending more time outside, walking and biking, is a positive goal. You can be *against* animal cruelty, but you can be *for* shelter adoption. You can be *against* factory farms, but you can be *for* eating local, organic, or vegetarian.

To really get involved in a cause, you have to be aware of the negative forces creating the problem as well as passionately devoted to positive action, or you probably won't last very long. Activists who stay positive and maintain a sense of humor but also stick stubbornly to their convictions in the face of opposition are likelier to get attention and accomplish more for their causes than the humorless, angry types who seem to focus only on the negative. And being a positive activist is a lot more rewarding. Sure, anger is a powerful motivator, but it wears you down after a while.

In other words, to be an activist, you can't just *care*. You have to care enough to do something, in a way that taps your own skills and keeps you motivated. There are many different causes that make it easy to get involved, so consider whether any of the following situations really light a fire under you.

Animal abuse: Are you devastated by the knowledge that people fight dogs and roosters, hoard pets, and abuse animals in other ways? Do you feel the need to help stop it by increasing awareness or helping to encourage state and local officials to improve laws?

Animal rescue: Are you devoted to a particular kind of animal? Would you like to do what you can to provide foster care or help for organizations that rescue those animals? Could you help with the transport of rescued animals, or would you want to work at an animal sanctuary?

Anticonsumerism: Are you opposed to the worship of the almighty dollar? Would you like to see people stop buying stuff and instead return to simpler pleasures? Do you want to make anticonsumerism a way of life?

Factory farms: Are you horrified by what goes on behind slaughterhouse doors, as well as by the way farm animals are treated as they are being mass produced? Would you like to work in a farm animal sanctuary that rescues animals intended for slaughter?

Food: Would you love to see more people and animals eating organic? Local? Vegetarian or vegan? Can you think of good ways to spread the word or at least set a good example through your own actions and by patronizing local businesses that follow these principles?

Global warming: Are you passionate about our imperiled planet? Do you want to

Green Words

People's dreams are made out of what they do all day, the same way a dog that runs after rabbits will dream of rabbits. It's what you do that makes your soul, not the other way around.

—Barbara Kingsolver,
American author

raise awareness about global warming so we can begin to reverse it and maybe even save life on the planet?

Pet overpopulation: Are you concerned about the millions of animals being euthanized in animal shelters? Are you devoted to shelter adoption? To spreading the word about spaying and neutering pets? To assisting animal shelters with whatever they need?

Puppy mills: Do you hate the idea that dogs are mass produced, often in inadequate or cruel conditions, purely for profit? Do you want to stop it by raising awareness?

Recycling: Are you all about reducing trash, reusing what you or your family members already have, and recycling what you throw away? Does your community need help organizing or improving their recycling efforts?

Wildlife preservation: Would you like to contribute volunteer time or money to help save wild animals from habitat loss and the effects of pollution?

Green Fact

Animal welfare activists have been working to get the government to ban the cruel sport of cockfighting for years. As of August 15, 2008, when Louisiana passed a law banning the so-called sport, cockfighting is now officially illegal in all fifty states.

What Can You Do?

What would you really like to do, that would inspire you and energize you and encourage you to keep going? If it makes you uncomfortable to ask people for things, then you aren't going to enjoy being the one who solicits donations for an animal shelter, but you might love helping out in the cattery.

If you love to write, you might enjoy penning letters championing your cause to your members of Congress or to the local paper, but you might not want to be in the thick of things, handing out brochures on the street. Think about what kind of person you are and what you are good at.

Activist groups need plenty of help accomplishing a wide range of goals.

Volunteer at a Shelter

Animal shelters, sanctuaries, and rescue groups depend heavily on volunteers, and they almost always need more help. There are many ways you can contribute, from walking dogs, playing with cats, and cleaning cages to answering phones, processing paperwork, and editing their newsletters. Ask what they need, but also do what you are good at doing. Tell all your friends that you volunteer at a shelter, and encourage them to adopt their future animal companions from one.

To find shelters near you, visit the Web site www.pets911.com. Click on "Find Shelters & Rescues," and you will be able to choose between links to finding local shelters and rescues, finding local adoption locations, finding volunteer opportunities, and a lot more.

Green Tip

Some small communities don't have an animal shelter, and the police have to handle any animal control issues. If you think your community could benefit from an animal shelter, check out the publication *Animal Control Management: A Guide for Local Governments*, by Geoffrey L. Handy, published by the International City/County Management Association. It is available for eleven dollars from the Humane Society of the United States and contains information for individuals or local governments that are seeking to set up, fund, and run an effective animal care and control program. To order this publication, you should contact the Humane Society's Animal Sheltering program: 2100 L Street NW, Washington, DC 20037, (202) 452-1100, www.animalsheltering.org.

Provide a Foster Home

Rescue groups always need more foster homes. These homes take in newly rescued pets while the group seeks permanent homes for them. Whenever you foster an animal, you do a good deed. Yet you also need to know how to deal with and help evaluate animals that may have some temporary or permanent problems that could be the cause of, or the result of, their abandonment. Are you the kind of person who can handle the responsibility? Do you have, or can you get, the knowledge and training necessary?

Ask your local animal shelter if it works with any rescue groups needing foster help, or contact local rescue groups directly. The Web site www.pets911.com has a link to finding fostering opportunities and a whole section all about fostering pets. Go to www.pets911.com/services/foster/fostering_orgs.php, and enter your zip code to find local foster care needs.

You can also find local rescues and animal welfare groups on Petfinder. Go to www.petfinder.com and enter your zip code in the area that says "Find Animal Welfare Groups," and you'll get a handy list with links and phone numbers. Just call the organizations near you to ask whether they need volunteers.

Volunteer at a Park

National parks and wildlife refuges also need volunteers. You might feed birds, clean pens, help maintain trails, help band birds, or assist in wildlife population surveys, or you could help in the office if you aren't the work-outdoors type. Many parks offer educational programs for schools and other groups, need help in their laboratories, or need help with their technical or administrative load. According to the National Park Service, 137,000 volunteers

donated 5.2 million hours to national parks in fiscal year 2005, and all that work was worth $91.2 million.

To find wildlife volunteer opportunities, contact your local refuge or nearby state or national parks or forests. You can also read more about volunteering at national parks and wildlife refuges on the sites for the National Park Service (www.nps.gov/volunteer/) and the U.S. Fish and Wildlife Services (www.fws.gov/volunteers/).

Quit!

No, this probably isn't the time to quit your job. However, for a predetermined time (or indefinitely), there are plenty of other things you can quit to eco-friendly effect. For example, you could quit driving, buying anything made overseas, watching television, buying anything new, generating any nonrecyclable waste, or eating all animal products. Tell people why you are doing it.

If you quit doing something that most people do, you are going to attract attention; when you do (or even if you don't) tell people why you have quit. You might get people arguing with you, but you will also raise awareness. If you like to do this sort of thing, you can be an activist without actually joining a group. Start a blog or write an article about your experience.

If you research your issue and have a handy list of answers and facts, you can explain your motivation to people more effectively. For example, if you decide to quit eating animal products, you might need some information to answer questions about the health, animal welfare, and environmental impact of a vegan diet.

Leave Flyers and Brochures

Leave flyers and brochures in strategic places wherever you go. Many organizations provide free promotional material that you can hand out or leave lying around. But don't litter!

Give Talks

Give talks at local schools about the best ways to treat animals or how to be a responsible pet parent. Schools love to promote programs that include animals. If you have the credentials and can organize an entertaining presentation to help teach kids how to treat animals, the environment, or both, local schools will probably be interested. Kids are very willing to learn about animal care as well as earth care.

Write Letters to Officials

Writing to your local and national politicians really does make a difference. They actually read those letters, and it is an easy way to get involved in causes that matter to you. Congressional staffers notice when they receive ten or more letters from their

GREEN RESOURCES

Do you need more information about vegetarianism or veganism and why it is better for health, animals, and the environment? Check out the following resources:

🔥 *Compassion over Killing:* www.cok.net. This nonprofit group is devoted to animal advocacy. It works to end animal abuse, and it champions a vegetarian diet as an important way to end animal and human cruelty as well as global warming for a cleaner and more compassionate world. For more information, see Resources, "Animal Welfare Resources."

🔥 *Vegetarian Resource Group:* www.vrg.org. This nonprofit group is "dedicated to educating the public on vegetarianism and the interrelated issues of health, nutrition, ecology, ethics, and world hunger." It publishes the *Vegetarian Journal* as well as many books, pamphlets, and article reprints. See Resources, "Green Organizations."

🔥 *VegWeb:* www.vegweb .com. A great source of vegetarian recipes.

🔥 *Vegetarian-Restaurants .net:* www.vegetarian-restau rants.net. Enter your state, and find vegetarian and vegetarian-friendly restaurants near you.

constituents about a particular issue. Don't just copy a form letter, although you can get ideas from one. If the letter is unique, it will garner more attention.

If you do write to your local officials or state representatives or senators, be sure to follow up on how they vote on the issues, write them thank-you notes, or continue to solicit their attention, and be sure to remind them after election day how you voted and why. Send your letters to any of the following addresses:

The name of your Representative
U.S. House of Representatives
Washington, DC 20515

The name of your Senator
U.S. Senate
Washington, DC 20510

President
The White House
1600 Pennsylvania Avenue NW
Washington, DC 20500

You can also contact your senators and your representative through their Web sites: For the U.S. Senate, go to www.senate .gov/contacting/index.cfm, find your state, and click on a senator; you'll be sent right to his or her Web page, where you can find further contact information. For the House of Representatives, go to https://writerep .house.gov, find your state in the drop-down list, enter your zip code, and get a ready-made e-mail you can use to send a letter to the right person. Call the U.S. Capitol at (202) 224-3121. Call the White House comment line at (202) 456-1111.

Write Letters to the Paper

If writing to politicians isn't for you, but you love to write and you'd rather speak directly to the people, try writing letters to your local newspaper. The editors don't print every letter, but they do typically print well-written letters that speak to issues of community interest. If your first letter doesn't get published, keep working on your writing skills and on expressing your thoughts clearly. Let helpful friends see your letter and offer you constructive criticism. Then, remain persistent, and keep an eye on the local news so that your letters are current and relevant.

Start a Blog

Start and publicize a blog devoted to your cause. These days, it's easy to start your own blog, and it's an effective way to share your thoughts with the world. A lot of sites offer free blogging space, such as www .blogger.com, www.wordpress.com, and www.livejournal.com. You don't have to know about Web site design or programming or anything other than how to click on a few setup instructions and start writing. The most popular blogs usually have a theme, such as updates on laws about pets, writing about your experiment to go one year without buying anything new, eating only local food, or seeing how many ways you can reduce your carbon footprint. You can publicize your blog by adding the address to your e-mail signature, by listing it on your business card, or just by mentioning it to people whenever you can.

If a blog is too ambitious, join a social networking site such as Facebook (www

Green Guidance

Find out what the politicians running your state and country really think based on how they have voted and what public statements they have made at Project Vote Smart, a self-proclaimed "factual, nonbiased" source of political information that calls itself "The Voter's Self-Defense System." Find it at www.votesmart .org. You can search by politician's last name or by your zip code to find out a lot of really interesting information.

.facebook.com), which lets you connect with other people who have similar interests and provides a venue to join groups devoted to your cause. On Twitter (www. twitter.com), you can post short messages to the world as often as you like and gain followers.

Organize a Protest

A peaceful protest is an excellent way to generate awareness in your community about an issue. Protests can be organized to object to a temporary local event (like an issue up for a vote or a passing circus that exploits animals), or it can be organized on the steps of city hall or another high-profile place regarding an ongoing issue (such as

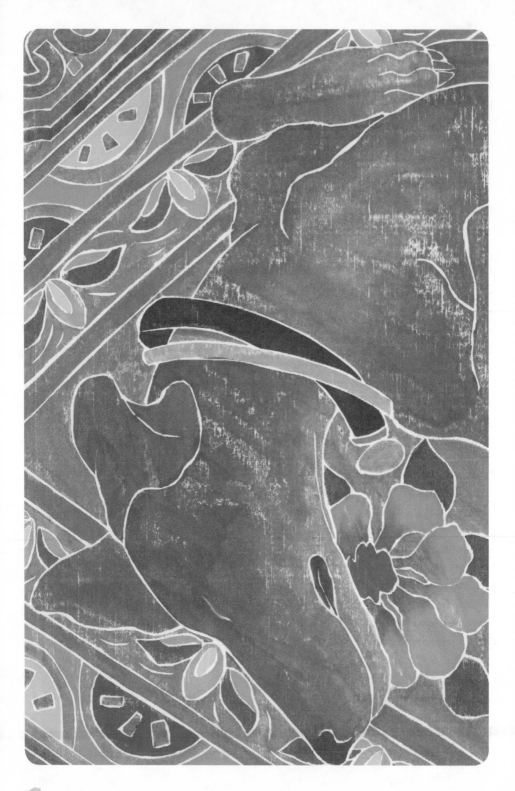

PETS GONE GREEN

animal cruelty or global warming). If you are involved with local groups related to your cause, you may have the occasional protest already organized. If you want to do it, consider the following actions.

Choose an effective protest site. Pick a highly visible place or a government office where officials will see you. But do not be confrontational or get in people's way.

Alert the media. Let local newspapers and television stations know about your protest, to increase the likelihood that they will cover it in the news. This will spread your message even more widely.

Have speakers. People speaking, even briefly, on the issue in an inspiring way can motivate others to take action.

Pass out literature. As you attract a crowd, you will have an opportunity to distribute information about your cause. (Use recycled paper!)

Hold a silent vigil. Sometimes, silence is more powerful than shouting. A silent vigil with signage to express your cause can be very effective. Animals can't speak, so if your protest is related to an animal cause, a silent vigil is particularly relevant. It also tends to keep people calmer.

Be prepared for law enforcement. Protests make people nervous, so if the local police hear about your protest, they may show up just to make sure nobody breaks any laws or things don't get out of hand. An effective protest does *not* have to break laws or get out of control.

Set a Good Example

Setting a good example may be the most important thing you can do. People are

GREEN RESOURCES

An eye-opening blog called *Green Is the New Red* tracks instances in the news of activists for environmental, animal-rights, antiwar, and other causes being targeted as so-called terrorists. The site focuses on "how fear of 'terrorism' is being exploited to push a political and corporate agenda." Specifically, it looks at "how animal-rights and environmental advocates are being branded 'eco-terrorists' in what many are calling the Green Scare." Do activists sometimes go too far? Probably, but go to this site and decide for yourself: www.greenisthenew red.com. It also has a link to the National Lawyers Guide "Green Scare Hotline" for any activist who has experienced harassment because of actual or perceived political beliefs: 1-888-NLG-ECOL.

attracted to interesting, happy, healthy, motivated people with a purpose. Stay healthy, and keep your animals healthy. Stay positive, focused, and out there. Let your activism make you a happier person, and everyone will want to know your secret. And then you can tell them.

Being an activist can be addictive because it adds passion and purpose to your life, and that feels good. However, activism also requires courage. If you believe in something, acting on those beliefs, living your values, and being the change you wish to see in the world really can make it a better place.

Chapter 8

Trash
Talk

Your

Environmental

Impact

Statement

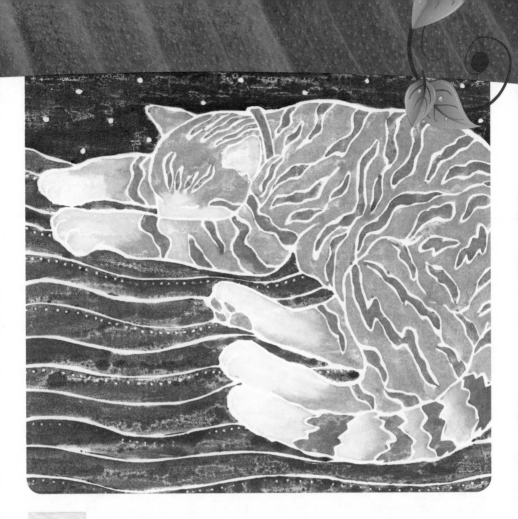

Let's talk trash. Americans generate a great deal of it. In fact, Americans produce about 4.4 pounds of garbage every single day. Some of that trash is directly related to our companion animals. They make waste that we dispose of in garbage bags. We also spray, squirt, and douse our homes with products that

are designed to remove pet odor and various pet stains.

We wash our companion animals (and ourselves) in products that are filled with chemicals, and we build our homes with materials that give off chemical gases as well. And that's not even mentioning all of the packaging that we throw away without a thought.

How can we reduce that giant carbon pawprint? The answer to that question is what this chapter is all about. We will focus on finding the least toxic and pollution-generating strategies for dealing with the serious issues of pet waste, pet odor, pet grooming needs, and that source of some of the most noxious chemicals of all, pest control.

Cat Poop: A Different Story

Dog poop is flushable, but cat poop is a different story. Up to half of all cats are infected by a parasite called *Toxoplasma gondii*. This parasite can sail through the sewage treatment plant processes unscathed and end up back in the water system, where it can be harmful to humans, especially pregnant women and people with compromised immunities. It has also been shown to be dangerous to wildlife, especially sea otters, many of which die from exposure to this parasite. A vet can do a litter test (a test that measures antibodies in blood) on your cat to see if he has this parasite, which is harmless to him) If your cat doesn't have it and never goes outside or eats any raw meat, you can flush your cat's poop, too. Otherwise, cat poop should never be flushed. Instead, it should be discarded via the trash or, better yet, composted (for use on nonfood gardens only, such as flowers) or buried in the soil, far away from any gardens that contain food crops, like your vegetable garden.

The Straight Poop

When my kids were a lot younger, a friend gave them the book *Everybody Poops* for some occasion. After we all got over the shock of the title and the artist's interesting renderings, the kids found the book highly amusing. It also speaks a frank truth. Everybody *does* poop, and all that poop has to go somewhere.

According to Christie Keith in her "Your Whole Pet" column on the *San Francisco Chronicle*'s Web site, dogs in America produce approximately 10 million tons of poop every year. Cats add 2 million tons of cat litter and waste to the mix, and all that poop and waste ends up in landfills. If this waste is left to lie around in the environment and washes into the groundwater, then the water that we all drink and use can become contaminated with dangerous bacteria.

Not that humans don't generate even more waste, but our sewage treatment plants are designed to process it in a safe way, using natural processes to biodegrade that waste back into the earth safely. Those treatment plants can process dog poop, too, so why are we throwing all our dog poop into landfills?

What a Waste

First, consider that nature is very good at cleaning itself. Forests and fields and the ocean aren't teeming with the contaminated poop of wild animals, are they? You may see the occasional pile of scat on a hike, but eventually insects and the natural cycle process that poop back into the earth, rendering the bacteria harmless.

But leave a pile of dog poop on a sidewalk, and that natural process is not going to work because the poop can't biodegrade on an impenetrable surface. Before the poop biodegrades, it is teeming with bacteria, and that puts everybody at risk, including your companion animals, which can pick up dangerous diseases from the poop of other dogs.

In any case, the law usually requires that you clean up after your dog. What happens when you scoop that poop into a plastic bag? A naturally biodegradable material is suddenly encased in a nonbiodegradable material, so that biodegradable poop sits inside a plastic bag for hundreds of years in a landfill without ever getting back into the soil. How stupid is that?

Enter the biodegradable poop bag. These bags biodegrade so the poop can do so, too, the way nature intended. Some landfills are so tightly packed that nothing degrades, but a biodegradable poop bag in a landfill is better than a plastic bag in a landfill. Even better, you can flush the flushable ones or compost them in your own yard this way (see the next section), or if your city has a biodegradable waste disposal service that allows pet waste, you can dispose of the bags there. (Call your city to be sure before you start throwing waste bags away.)

Biodegradable poop bags really are the only sensible way to work with the power of nature to keep the planet cleaner. If your local dog park or hiking trail provides poop bags but they are not biodegradable, make some calls and see whether you can change that. Get your friends to call, as well. The squeaky wheel gets the biodegradable poop bag. See the Resources, "Biodegradable Poop Bags, Cat Pan Liners, and Litter," for companies that are selling these bags.

The same problem applies to cat litter. In nature, cats scratch around in the dirt, poop, and bury the waste so the soil can decompose it safely. When cats poop in litter boxes, however, most people wrap the litter and poop in a plastic bag and put it in

Green Tip

There you are, walking your dog, steamy poop bag in hand. There it is: the sewer. While it might be tempting to just dump that biodegradable poop bag into the storm drain, stop! Don't do it. These drains typically go directly into local rivers and lakes. The effect of the waste on the water's natural ecosystem can be devastating. It causes ammonia spikes, reduced oxygen, warmer temperatures, and diseased organisms, which in turn can sicken or kill fish and other wildlife. This contaminated water can also put humans at risk when used for swimming.

the trash, to be carted off to a landfill where it cannot decompose.

And about that cat litter—did you ever wonder where it came from? Clay litter comes from strip mining, an incredibly environmentally destructive process. Because the clay is already at the end of a decomposition cycle, it isn't going to decompose any more, so it just sits there in landfills— stripped from the earth, then piled up on top of a bunch of trash. Ridiculous.

Some cat litter is biodegradable, however, offering a much better alternative. Like the biodegradable poop bags, it may or may not have ideal decomposition conditions in a landfill, but if you throw it away in a paper bag instead of last-forever plastic, you maximize the chances that it

will go back to the earth. Better yet, you can compost it (see the next section).

The biodegradable litters I've seen are made out of wheat, corn, pine, or old newspapers. Many handle odor just as well as, if not better than, traditional clay and clumping litters. The problem is that some cats used to clay litter don't like the feel of different litter. The best way to teach your stubborn kitty to be more environmentally minded is to replace just a small amount of the old litter with the new. Every time you change the litter, increase the amount of the new litter a bit, gradually seducing your cat into a new eco-friendly way of life.

Some people recommend biodegradable cardboard litter boxes, and these are fine for traveling purposes, but throwing away litter box after litter box generates more trash. Instead, get a long-lasting litter box that you can use for your cat's entire life, and maybe for your next few cats, too. Fill the box with biodegradable litter.

A few brands of biodegradable cat litter that I like:

Swheat Scoop: www.swheatscoop.com, (800) 794-3287. Unlike clay litters, this natural wheat litter is renewable, completely biodegradable, and great at nixing litter box odor via natural wheat enzymes. Produced from naturally processed secondary wheat, this not only is an environmentally friendly product but also contains no dust and is safe and nontoxic for cats and kittens, even if ingested.

Feline Pine: www.naturesearth.com. This is the litter made from recycled wood dust and remnants, which the company reclaims from lumberyards. The company forms the

pine dust into pellets, but the litter itself is dust free and completely natural—and the Feline Pine Scoop variety even clumps.

World's Best Cat Litter: www.worldsbest catlitter.com. This brand is also flushable (but, again, composting is better) and it is made from whole-kernel corn, which has a microporous structure that the company says traps and absorbs odor without any added chemicals or perfumes. It is completely safe and dust free and won't harm cats if they accidentally ingest some of it.

Yesterday's News: www.yesterdaysnews .com. This litter is made from recycled newspapers, and the company says their manufacturing process neutralizes ink residue so the product is nontoxic. This litter is not flushable. Fill the litter box with just two or three inches. This litter absorbs from the bottom so you want to change it often and keep an eye on what is going on at the bottom level of litter.

PlanetWise Products: www.planetwise products.com. This company makes all-natural pine pellet litter in regular and clumping formulas for cats, as well as pine pellet bedding for horse stalls, small animal enclosures, and bird enclosures. Several sources advise against using pine shavings for small animals because they can be linked to respiratory problems, but this company's Cozy 'n Fresh product is sterile and has all the aromatic hydrocarbons and irritating oils removed, so it's perfectly safe.

Composting Pet Waste

I'm a diehard composter. I have a big compost pile beside my deck, enclosed in what used to be an hexagonal plastic "play yard" for dogs and puppies. Every day I throw all my kitchen scraps, coffee grounds, and any other food waste in there (except meat, bones, dairy, or oil, which can attract some serious vermin). As many composters have in the past, I often wondered, why can't I just compost pet waste?

Actually, I can, and so can you—*if* you follow some safety rules. Pet waste, and the waste of any other animals (including humans) that eat meat, is likely to contain some nasty bacteria, including *E. coli* and

Salmonella. (I will refrain here from adding another shameless plug about not eating meat.) Not exactly what you want to use to feed your vegetable garden, is it? However, you can feed your flowers and trees with the stuff.

There are two good ways to compost pet waste. One is to create two compost piles. Use one for your vegetable garden and one for the areas of your yard that don't produce things you will eat. Don't put them side by side. They could be, for example, in separate corners of the yard. A pet compost pile should also be at least 100 yards from any water source.

Add dog waste, with or without biodegradable bags; cat poop; biodegradable cat litter; and the waste from any other animals you have, such as the newspapers covered in bird poop in your bird's enclosure or the litter from your rabbit's, guinea pig's, or other small animal's pen. Every time you add some poop, cover it up with green material such as grass clippings or leaves, or green food scraps. Then, let nature take its course.

The other way to compost is to build a pet waste disposal system. This is actually fairly easy to do and doesn't take any fancy equipment other than a shovel and a strong back. This project lets pet waste biodegrade and then "melt" back into the soil of your yard when it is free of harmful bacteria. It's amazing, actually. It takes full advantage of nature's natural cleaning methods. To set up your own system, see the box on the next page.

Once you have built the system, whenever you have pet waste, toss it in. The

Green Facts

The inner core and outer fibers of sustainable, renewable hemp make an excellent, safe, clean, dust-free, antimicrobial, absorbent bedding material for rabbits and other small animals as well as for birds and horses. Canadian-based NuHemp makes a product called BIO-Nesting out of the hemp plant. Check it out at www.nuhemp.com.

Building a
Backyard Disposal System

I found out how to build a pet waste disposal system on the City Farmer Web site at www.cityfarmer.org:

- Cut the bottom off of a large plastic garbage can. Drill holes all over the sides of the garbage can.
- Dig a hole in your yard the size of the can. Put the can in the hole. Fill the hole with about 6 inches of gravel or rocks in the bottom.
- Put on the lid, which should be approximately level with the grass. You might want to label it something like "Pet Waste Only."
- The first time you put pet waste in the can, also put in some septic system starter, which you can buy at the hardware store, and some water. The starter urges waste to start decomposing quickly.

To see good photos and videos on how to do this, check out the City Farmer Web site. It also has great information on other kinds of composting including worm composting, gardening, lawn care, and rain barrels.

waste will degrade naturally and trickle down through the gravel back into the soil when it is ready. Add more septic starter every so often, perhaps once a month, depending on how much waste is in the can.

Occasionally throw in some dead leaves or grass clippings to encourage the composting process. Mixing it all in together will help, too, because it will get more air into the deeper layers, which speeds up the decomposition. If you don't want to do that, however, it's not absolutely necessary.

The pet waste will turn into compost before it rinses back down into the soil, so you can also open it up and use that compost on flowers and trees. Remember, though, just to be safe—don't put it on your vegetable garden.

You can also make a pet waste disposal system by just digging a hole, without the garbage can, but this is more likely to cave in and typically holds less waste.

Banishing Odor and Stains Naturally

Everybody poops, but animals living in human homes sometimes poop in the wrong place. And pee. And throw up. All those lovely things. Of course you want to keep your house clean, sweet smelling, and stain free, and this is entirely possible without dousing every stain and little "accident" with chemicals.

Natural enzymes and other substances from plants have the remarkable ability to destroy odor molecules. Rather than

masking odors or removing just the top layers of a stain, many of the newer natural stain and odor control products actually do a really good job—in certain cases, a much better job than chemical products are capable of.

Green Products to Treat Odors and Stains

Look for products that contain natural botanical ingredients and plant-based enzymes rather than those with ingredients that have long, scary-looking chemical names you don't recognize. These are far superior to stain and odor removers filled with nasty chemicals that can irritate eyes, skin, and lungs. A few of my favorites are listed here.

Fresh Wave: www.fresh-wave.com. It's hard to believe how well this company's sprays, gels, vacuum pearls, candles, and cleaning fluids work. (I swear the company is not paying me to say that!) These products are made by a company with a long history of odor control in industrial environments, so it has had to invent ways to deal with odor far beyond anything your dog or cat could cough up. The products have only a few natural ingredients, and they eliminate odor like nothing else that I have ever tried.

Earth Friendly Products: www.ecos .com. This company makes products for the whole house, and it never tests its products on animals; these products contain no animal ingredients. The cleaners are totally plant based, and Earth Friendly Products uses only recycled paper. Their animal-relevant products include an excellent stain- and odor-removing product, a laundry detergent for your companion animal's clothes and bedding, a spray for skin and coat that removes body odor and can even reduce allergic reactions in people sensitive to pet dander, pet wipes for paws, a natural chew-deterrent spray, a skunk odor remover, a kitty litter treatment formula, and a cleaner for your bird's enclosure.

Petrotech: www.sea-yu.com. Based in San Francisco, this company makes a nitrogen-propelled odor eliminator that won't damage the ozone and is nontoxic and completely biodegradable. Petrotech is rigorous about its process and also about using environmentally friendly packaging. For more information on the company, see Resources, "Green Odor/Stain Control Products."

Other Products for Odors and Stains

You can also tackle stains with some of the products you have in your own kitchen and bathroom. Treat stains as soon as possible

Green Terms

When scanning the ingredients on natural and organic grooming products, you may see the term *saponified*. That just means "made into soap," through exposure to an alkali (a base, such as lye). For example, saponified olive oil is olive oil made into soap.

for best results. Try using the home remedies listed below.

For pet pee stains: Blot up as much moisture as you can with a dry towel. Put a few drops of castile soap on the spot and scrub with a wet cloth or brush, then rinse with a mixture of vinegar in water in a 1:8 ratio. Cover with towels, and weight them to absorb the moisture (I usually just step on the towels for a minute or two).

For pet vomit stains: Get as much vomit off the carpet as possible with paper towels or a washcloth. Pour club soda on the stain and let sit for five minutes. Cover with dry towels, and weight them to absorb moisture (again, standing on them for a minute or two works great).

For general deodorizing: Sprinkle baking soda on carpets, rugs, or pet bedding, and let sit for about ten minutes. Vacuum, wash, or shake out.

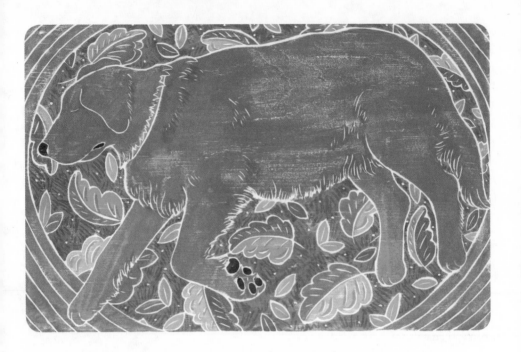

Earth-Friendly and Pet-Friendly Grooming

It's fairly obvious why you would want to feed your animals (and yourself) organic food, but the good reasons for using organic and all-natural grooming products may be less obvious. Most shampoos, whether made for companion animals or for people, contain chemicals. Many people and pets have skin problems. Is there a connection? Skin is permeable, and what we put on our skin soaks into our bodies.

In a healthy person or animal, the effects of chemical sudsing agents, preservatives, and artificial colors and fragrances are probably minimal. In a person or animal with immune system problems, allergies, or other health issues, however, grooming can cause severe skin irritation. Some holistic veterinarians even believe there is a link between toxic chemical exposure (of all kinds) through the skin and cancer in companion animals.

You might have heard that you shouldn't bathe your pets too often because doing so irritates the skin. In many cases, however, that irritation comes from the sudsing agents and other chemical ingredients rather than from the bathing itself. Use a less irritating, all-natural shampoo, and you should have few, if any, problems, even in healthy people and pets, chemical exposure could have a cumulative effect.

Grooming products made with natural botanicals and without harmful chemicals are gentler on skin, but organic products are gentler still, Plants in natural products free of pesticides won't leave that toxic residue on your pet. Dr.. Shawn Messonnier, a holistic veterinarian and the author of many books on holistic health care for companion animals, including the *Natural Health*

Bible for Dogs and Cats, recommends the following when choosing a pet shampoo:

- 🔥 No DEA or TEA
- 🔥 No parabens
- 🔥 No sodium laurel sulfate, sodium lauryl sulfate, or any other sulfate
- 🔥 No alcohol
- 🔥 No phosphates
- 🔥 No detergents
- 🔥 No dyes
- 🔥 pH balanced
- 🔥 No pesticides (i.e., the product should be organic)
- 🔥 No plastic bottles made with BPA
- 🔥 Cruelty free (i.e., not tested on animals)

Organic, chemical-free, cruelty-free grooming products are not only safer and probably healthier for companion animals (and people, too) but also better for the environment, all the way down the supply chain. Buying organic grooming products supports the farmers who produce the plants that go into the products, and once again you are voting with your dollars to promote the production of personal products that don't harm.

The problem with organic grooming products is that the industry isn't well regulated. The FDA doesn't regulate the term *organic* when it is applied to cosmetics, body care, or personal care products, including grooming products for animals. However, the USDA does regulate the term *organic* when applied to food products. If a grooming product manufacturer wants to put "USDA-certified Organic" on the label, it has to follow the USDA's standards as they

apply to food: a product must contain more than 70 percent but less than 95 percent organic ingredients to claim to be "made with organic ingredients." Another problem is compliance; some companies will try to get away with any label claim they think will sell more product. Before choosing a grooming product, look into the company. Look at their Web site, or call and ask about what really is in the products and what kind of quality-control measures are in place.

According to the Organic Trade Association, better regulation of grooming products for companion animals may be on the horizon. The current regulations were developed several decades ago for human food and beverage products, and they need updating now that organic and other natural products are in so much demand. Until that day, however, buyer beware.

Bug Free, Naturally

Perhaps no other animal-related problem tempts the well-intentioned environmentalist to use chemicals more than an infestation of fleas. Your companion animal may pick up a few fleas from an encounter with some buddies at the dog park, the neighbor's dog, or infested wildlife, but those fleas multiply fast, and they can be difficult to kill.

The misuse of flea and tick products is one of the leading causes of pet poisoning, according to the ASPCA, especially during the summer. That's not surprising, as flea and tick products *are* poison—that's how they kill bugs. If you don't want to put poison on your companion animals, get it on your own hands, or wash it down the drain, consider the eco-friendly and animal-friendly (but not bug-friendly!) alternatives.

The most important thing to do when you first find a flea, or evidence of a flea, on any of your companion animals, is to take action. Pick off the flea and drown it. No chemicals required. In fact, chemical control of those little suckers is overkill if you aren't facing an infestation. Nip fleas in the bud, and you never will. Better yet, practice prevention and you may never see a flea. Neither one of my dogs has ever had a flea problem, and I plan to keep it that way. In this section is your flea attack and prevention plan.

Grooming to Control Fleas

What's wrong with a little elbow grease? Nothing, I say. If you want the fleas off your pets, take the fleas off your pets! At least once every week, when brushing and combing your pet, work through the coat with a fine-toothed steel comb looking for fleas or flea dirt. Flea dirt looks like little black specks that turn red if you get them wet. That's because they are digested

blood. (I know, disgusting.) Perform your hunt daily if you find a flea.

If you find a flea, drop it in a little cup of rubbing alcohol. Don't just pick it off and throw it somewhere. Flea shells are strong and they are hard to squish, so the flea will probably just hop around on your carpet for a while, maybe lay some eggs, and then jump back on the nearest mammal.

But you can do more. A weekly bath goes a long way toward pest control. Fleas can hold their breath for a while, but they're not aquatic. If you bathe your dog or cat weekly and douse those fleas with plain old-fashioned water, then wash them down the drain, they don't stand a chance.

When you wash your dog or cat to remove fleas, the kind of shampoo you use can make a difference in how quickly the bugs want to jump off the gravy train. Give your animal a weekly bath in a gentle bug-repelling shampoo containing neem oil. Neem oil is an amazing substance that comes from the neem tree, which is native to India. Although companies that use neem oil in their products can't officially say that it kills bugs (this gets into a whole pesticide-approval mess of government red tape), my sources inform me that with regular use the oil can kill bugs, and it certainly repels fleas, which will seek friendlier (that is, less healthy and more vulnerable) skin to bite.

My favorite neem oil product comes from Ark Naturals, a Naples, Florida, company that also makes treats, supplements, and lots of other goodies. The shampoo they make is called Neem Protect Shampoo. They also make a Neem Protect spray.

Neem also is incredibly healing for the skin, so if your animal already has a few flea bites, putting neem oil on them will help prevent itching and further injury. Tea tree oil is another good natural botanical that soothes irritated and itchy skin. Both neem oil and tea tree oil also have antibacterial and anti-inflammatory properties.

For some dogs, a flea bite is no big deal. For others, it can cause serious problems, especially if the dog is allergic to fleas. These dogs can damage their own skin by scratching, developing wounds and hot spots—weepy, itchy sores they just can't stop licking and scratching. These sores can get seriously infected and need treatment, so if your animal develops a hot spot, talk to your vet about the best, safest approach.

Housekeeping to Control Fleas

Don't forget the house. Fleas only spend a small part of their life cycles on a mammal. Most of the time, they creep around in the grass or, if inside, in your carpet, on your pet's bedding, and on your furniture. Sure, you could bug bomb your house with poison, but why would you want to do that when all you have to do is break out the trusty vacuum cleaner?

Vacuum *daily* if you've actually spotted any fleas and at least weekly during flea season in any case; fleas won't get a foothold. Vacuum all carpets thoroughly, and use an attachment to vacuum all cushioned furniture and pet furniture. Some natural pet care sources suggest sprinkling borate crystals in the carpet because they

Green Guidance

Ticks need a more aggressive approach than basic bathing and combing. When a tick attaches itself to your pet, you need to take it off as quickly as possible. The longer ticks stay attached, the more chance they have to transmit serious diseases such as Lyme disease and Rocky Mountain spotted fever. But be careful. If the tick bursts, you are exposed to the fluid, putting you at risk, too. Always remove ticks while wearing rubber gloves or use a paper towel or tweezers. Pull the tick straight up and out, rather than yanking to the side, so no mouth parts break off underneath your animal's skin. If that happens anyway, despite your best efforts, keep an eye on the area. If it gets red and looks infected, call your veterinarian. Drop the tick into a small cup of rubbing alcohol to kill it, then throw it away.

PETS GONE GREEN

dry out the fleas, but this can also cause a lot of dust that pets can inhale. Instead, look for natural herbal carpet powders deemed safe for animals and children.

Vacuuming even without any products is fairly effective. Always throw away the vacuum bag immediately after using it. Seal it in a plastic bag, and put it in the outside trash. This is one area where it's OK to throw something away, sealed in plastic. You don't want those fleas to get out of the bag.

Utilize your trusty washing machine, too. Throw all washable parts of your animal's bed and bedding into the wash at least every week. Washing on cold saves energy, which is fine for clothes, but with pet bedding, to kill fleas, you should wash and dry at the highest heat setting. In addition, throw any soft toys, pet apparel, collars, and other products made of soft material into the wash (be sure items are washable). Cleanliness is next to buglessness and absolutely essential in arresting flea infestation in a nontoxic way.

Outside, keep grass mowed, and don't kill the ants in your yard. Ants feast on flea larvae and flea eggs.

Pest Control from the Inside Out

One of the most overlooked ways to prevent bugs from latching on is to make sure your companion animals are healthy. Bugs look for the easiest targets: the weakest animals with the most sensitive skin. Healthy animals with supple, strong skin aren't as appealing. Feed your animals a high-quality diet, and think about supplementing with essential fatty acids, such as those in

Green Guidance

When dogs or cats play outside, you can minimize the chance that fleas, ticks, and mosquitoes carrying diseases (deadly heartworms, tapeworms, avian influenza) will jump on for a ride if you spray your pet's coat lightly with an essential oil or herbal formula that repels bugs. Look for natural botanical insect repellents without any chemical names you don't recognize and that contain safe essential oils such as neem, tea tree, peppermint, citrus, or eucalyptus, or fragrant herbs in scents bugs hate, such as cedarwood, calendula, and rosemary. You can also spray any of these oils on a bandana or collar to put around your pet's neck, or you can look for herbal flea collars. (Conventional flea collars contain highly toxic pesticides.)

fish oil, flaxseed oil, and hemp oil. Make sure they get plenty of exercise. Just as important, reduce stress in your animals' lives by reducing stress in *your* life. You will feel better, your animals will feel calmer, everybody's immune system will work more efficiently, and the bugs might just decide to take their business elsewhere. Everybody wins.

Chapter 9

Green

Can Be Fun

It's Easy

Being

Green

very time I get ready to leave the house, Jack and Sally look at me with such anticipation, as if hoping beyond hope that I might just take them along (their expressions are adorable—I wish you could see them!). Whether I'm going for a walk in the woods, driving through the bank where they give out free

dog treats, or just picking the kids up from school, Jack and Sally want to come along.

When I go into my son's room to check on Grace, our cockatiel, she often hunkers down and lifts her wings up and bounces up and down, her birdy way of expressing to me that she very much wants me to pick her up, put her on my shoulder, and let her step all over my keyboard while I'm trying

to type something. (She added more than a few strange sentences to this book, which I've had to go back and delete.)

Our companion animals want to be with us, and although sometimes I wonder why (are we really that interesting?), I guess that's the reason we call them our companions. We are all products of centuries of mutual admiration and evolution. Now, when the earth needs us, maybe we can all help together.

In fact, there are a lot of ways that you and your companion animals can work together to live a more eco-friendly existence and have fun doing it. Hey, I know. Let's devote an entire chapter to the concept! I'm going to dispense with all the *don't do this* and *don't do that* and *for Pete's sake never do that other thing*. Let's be good activists and focus on the positive. Let's talk about how to have fun with your companion animals in way that makes it really easy to be green.

Green Sweet Home

To a companion animal, home means everything. Animals depend on routines and familiarity. Their dens mean safety and security, and their families, if they take good care of one another, become the pack, the clan, the tribe—the very essence of home. Spending time at home with your companion animals is a way to bond with them and also to luxuriate in everything home means to you. Staying home has environmental benefits as well. It means you aren't out driving your car or buying more stuff. (Yes, you can buy stuff at home on the Internet, but at least for the time it takes to read this chapter, see if you can refrain.)

If your home is a green home—meaning energy efficient and producing less waste than does the average home—the time you spend there will be even nicer because you will know you are making

Green Words

> Home, home,
> Strayed ones home,
> Rabbit to burrow,
> Fox to earth,
> Mouse to the wainscot,
> Rat to the barn,
> Cattle to the byre,
> Dog to the hearth,
> All beasts home!
>
> —Kathleen Raine,
> British poet, *The Year One* (1952)

a positive impact on your environment. This isn't about giving up good things—it's about finding them.

Having Fun and Conserving Resources

First, consider how you spend your time at home. Whether you come home to your animals or with your animals, you can do a lot of things to conserve energy and resources and live a simpler, more joyful life.

Turn things off. Turn off the television, the computer, the satellite radio, and the cell phones, and talk to your family. Look people and animals in the eye. Touch one another. Slow down and hang out.

Play music. Many animals love music. Our cockatiel, Grace, bobs her head up and down, dancing to songs she likes. (She ignores the songs she doesn't like or squawks about them. Or maybe she is singing along.) When everybody in the family ends up dancing in the living room, they are making some seriously good memories, getting exercise, and warming up the house without turning up the heat.

Turn down the heat. Turn down the thermostat, and let your animals sleep with you. A bed full of people and animals is a warm bed.

Design cozy dog spots. Design spots around the house for animals to hang out. You don't have to buy a fancy dog bed. Soft, washable fleece or faux fur blankets draped on your dog's or cat's favorite couch or chair feel comfortable and comforting, and you will have less pet hair on the furniture. Just throw the special blanket in the wash once a week.

Fill up the toy box from home. Fill up your dog's or cat's toy box without spending a dime by making your own pet toys instead of buying them. *However,* be safe. Socks, underwear, and panty hose are three of the most commonly ingested items that veterinarians must surgically remove from pets, so don't let pets play with these toys unsupervised. That goes for purchased pet toys, too, if they have pieces that can be broken, chewed, or ripped off and swallowed. Not all dogs chew up toys in this way, but if you have a chewer, take away the toy after you have finished playing with or supervising your dog.

Stuff an old sock with crumpled paper (and maybe a bit of catnip), and sew or tie the end for a tug toy or comfort toy. Tie an old pair of panty hose into knots every few inches for a fun tug toy.

Cut old towels, pieces of fleece, baby blankets, denim jeans, or T-shirts into long strips, and then braid them into a tug toy,

Green Tip

If your kids have old stuffed toys they don't play with anymore and you don't mind teaching your dog that it's OK to chew on and carry around a stuffed animal, go ahead and recycle these toys into dog toys. However, don't use any toys with small plastic parts, such as eyes or bows, that could come off. If your dog swallows them, he could choke or suffer an internal injury.

tying them off at each end. Hemp fabric is digestible, so it's the safest choice, if you happen to have it.

Tie a few strings or pieces of yarn securely from a stick or knitting needle and tie feathers and bells on the ends, for a homemade cat teaser. (Be sure your cat doesn't play with this unattended. String can be dangerous if swallowed. Hemp string is digestible, so it's safer.)

Put a few pieces of healthy kibble, small treats, or blueberries (if your dog likes the berries) into an empty twenty-ounce soda bottle. Leave the cap off. Roll it to your dog.

Play Frisbee with the top of a plastic container. Or use a real Frisbee, if you already have one.

Crumple up a sheet of paper you were going to throw away. Crumple it tightly into a ball. Toss is to your cat. Anybody up for some empty toilet paper roll shredding? That's always fun.

Tie a long rope with knots in it from a tree limb so it hangs about one foot from the ground. Show your dog. Encourage him to tug it. My dog Jack has one of these, and he likes to shake it and growl and even jump up and hang from it. He's a strange little dog, but I bet other dogs would enjoy this game, too.

Turn on a flashlight. Point it at the floor in front of your cat (but do not shine the light in his eyes). Move the light. See if your cat thinks this is fun.

Making Your Home Greener

You can also tweak your home a little at a time, becoming gradually green rather than making big changes all at once. Consider some of these options as you need to re-stock and upgrade your home.

Turn off the lights. Can you turn off the lights and see just fine via natural sunlight?

Open the blinds and find out. Letting the sun in also keeps the house warmer in winter: free solar energy!

Delay turning on the air and the heat. See how long you can last without turning on the air conditioner in the summer. Memorial Day? June 1? Independence Day? Make a bet with another family to see who can last the longest. Who can go the longest in the winter without turning on the heat? October 1? Halloween? Thanksgiving? (Don't sacrifice animal health, however. Some animals, especially birds, some dogs, and small animals, are more sensitive to heat and cold. Be sure they have plenty of shelter, warm bedding, and the option of a nice spot in the sun or shade.)

Repair water and air leaks. Repair water leaks in the plumbing, insulate your pipes, and install low-flow showerheads, and you can potentially save a lot of water. Repair

air leaks around windows and doors to keep heat or air-conditioning inside. This is fairly easy to do with caulking or with weather stripping.

Do your own repairs. Do home repairs yourself instead of paying someone, if you can. Do-it-yourself projects not only save money but also make you feel more invested and involved in your home.

Maintain appliances. Keep major appliances clean and maintained so they work as efficiently as possible. When you need to replace your furnace, air-conditioning unit, water heater, or major appliances such as the refrigerator, freezer, stove, washer, and dryer, look into eco-friendly, energy-efficient options. They may cost more initially but will save you a lot of money over the long haul. Like other energy-efficient home options, some of these appliances may include government rebates, or you might be able to write off some of the cost on your taxes.

Install a pet door. A securely installed door to let pets in and out of the fenced yard decreases the number of times that you will have to open the door to let them out, letting out valuable heat or air-conditioning at the same time. Just be certain that the door doesn't leak when it is closed and that animals have a safe place to be when outside.

Plant trees and bushes. If you plant more trees and bushes around your house, they will serve as natural insulators.

Consider alternative energy sources. Look into adding solar panels (some companies will lease them to you), a wind turbine, or a geothermal heating and cooling system to help you consume less energy and use energy more efficiently at home. These technologies are more widely available than ever before, and some local communities will reimburse you for part of the cost. Talk to professional installers about the cost comparison and how soon these alternative energy sources will pay for themselves. You should also be able to write off a portion on your taxes.

Use green building materials. If you are adding on space to your home, consider green building materials made from sustainable materials like natural stone, handmade tile, bamboo, and cork.

Out and About

Dogs, and even some adventurous cats, are just waiting for you to take them outside. While not every city or town is set up for walking, or walking pets, walking a little more is good for you, good for your companion animals, and good for the earth. The more you get outside into the natural world, the more you will appreciate it, and that might just help inspire you to make more eco-friendly changes in your life. Here are some fun ways to get outside into the big world with your animals.

Check out local dog parks. These aren't great for all dogs, especially those that don't always get along with others, but for social butterflies they are like dog heaven. Get out there and let your dog run free in these safe fenced areas, but please follow all dog park rules and always check your pet for fleas when you get home. A good bath afterward, with a neem oil shampoo, couldn't hurt.

Walk around the block. Get to know the neighbors—human, canine, and feline—and you'll be teaching your dog more about the world. And why not walk to the store, to the bank, to the café? More outdoor cafés are allowing well-behaved dogs to join their human family members, European style. Some even sell dog treats.

Ride your bike. Athletic, larger dogs often enjoy learning to run alongside a bicycle. Or consider getting a basket or pet carrier made for a bike. Your small dog or cat can ride along.

Plant a garden. Raising your own organic vegetables brings you in direct contact with the earth, puts healthful food on the table, and gets you outside with your pets. In fact, some dogs are very skilled at helping you dig holes for seeds or bulbs. (That doesn't mean they won't dig them back up.) If you have a cat, consider adding a patch of catnip.

Keep farm animals. How much of a farmer would you like to be? Depending on ordinances in your area, you might be able to keep chickens, ducks, or goats as pets (and as a potential source of eggs or milk). If your own companion animals are not likely to get along with these additions to the family, however, then you had better keep those hobby farm dreams in your head for the present.

Make it easy for other animals to pay a visit to your home. Bring more birds into your yard by hanging bird feeders and keeping them full of seeds, especially during extreme temperatures and in the spring and fall when birds are migrating. Some birds like food spread across the ground or on the railings of the deck, which is easier for them to access than a small feeder. We fill our feeders and always sprinkle more seed along the deck railings; all the neighborhood birds like to hang out at our house. Add a hummingbird feeder, and get the thrill of watching these tiny birds suck out the nectar. Birds also need water, so keep a bird bath or small fountain clean and filled with fresh water at all times. A bird bath warmer will keep the water available during cold months.

Turn your yard into a wildlife refuge. You can attract wildlife to your yard in many ways, such as providing brush and cover for nesting, plenty of trees, and plants that produce berries and seeds birds like (in keeping with local and neighborhood ordinances, of course). Be aware, however, that if you urge wildlife to come into your yard, you cannot easily pick and choose which critters come and which don't. You might attract raccoons and hawks instead of bunnies and cardinals. Be prepared for encounters between wildlife and your dogs and cats.

One of the best ways to attract wildlife to your yard is to add a water source, like a fountain or a pond with plants and/or fish. In our goldfish pond, we've seen mating dragonflies, frogs, a huge variety of birds, and even the occasional raccoon. Keep water clean and moving with a pump and filter to discourage mosquitoes.

When You Must Drive

You can't walk everywhere. But these days you never know where the fluctuating gas prices will go next. Are they going up? Are they going down? No matter what, if you are in the market for a new vehicle, you have a lot of choices. If you travel frequently with your animals, a vehicle that provides enough safe space for them is an important consideration, but also consider an eco-friendly and animal-friendly alternative. (You will also want to look for pet-friendly hotels, recreational areas, even restaurants, and visit them with your animals. Check out Pets Welcome at www.petswelcome.com, which lists more than 1,800 pet-friendly hotels and features travel tips, for more information. And see the Resources section of this book.)

Fuel Conscious

What will power your next car? One of the most popular and high-profile eco-friendly options is the hybrid car. Hybrid cars use both gas and electricity for power. They get better gas mileage than regular gas-powered cars, and they produce less pollution. Just a few years ago, there were only a couple of options, but now most major auto manufacturers have gotten in on the hybrid

action, and the automobiles are getting more comfortable as well as more attractive. You can get a small hybrid car or even a hybrid SUV.

Electric cars are an exciting alternative. They don't use any gasoline; the drawback is that they don't go as far or as fast as other cars. Electric cars run on fuel cells (batteries) that you have to charge, and the average electric car can go for about 40 miles on a charge, so they are best for in-town driving. Electric cars are mostly still very small because a lighter weight allows the car to go longer on a charge. Expect

electric car technology to advance quite a bit in the near future.

Even gas-powered cars have their eco-friendlier options. Smaller cars and cars with higher fuel efficiency and lower emissions are kinder to the earth. What option you choose with a car depends on what you can afford, what you like, and how much you drive. And remember, *not buying* is eco-conscious, too. If your car still works fine, sometimes it's better to keep driving it than to buy something else. Can you wait a little longer to buy that new "green" technology?

PETS GONE GREEN

Green Tip

I have a Honda Element, a great car for dogs. A lot of people out there seem to agree. DogCars .com, a car-buying Internet resource created by veterinarian Dr. Marty Becker, of *Good Morning America* fame, and syndicated columnist Gina Spadafori, chose the Honda Element as the Dog-Car of the Year in 2007. This spacious car with its clamshell doors is easy to get in and out of and easy to clean. You can add a lot of accessories to it, as you need them, and it can be custom-fitted for outdoor activities such as hiking, camping, skiing, surfing, and biking. So this car will inspire you to get out into the natural world more often, with or without your companion animals. It is a low-emission vehicle that gets good gas mileage for its size, so it's eco-friendly in that way, too. It's also fun to drive and a great car for families with kids.

Pet Friendly

If you travel with your animals, consider whether the car is low enough for them to get into unassisted, or whether you can add a ramp or steps, especially for larger dogs that are hard to lift and may be suffering from arthritis or hip problems. Can your animal's travel crates fit in the car safely, and can they be buckled in? What kind of seat material is easiest to clean, and which kind attracts pet hair like a magnet?

Spending Time Together

When you spend more time, at home or on the road, with your animals, they really will inspire you to lead a simpler, more natural life, so include them more often in the things you do. Pay attention to them. Notice when their behavior changes or how they are feeling. Get to know their personalities, and appreciate their quirks. When your companion animals become more integrated into your daily life, you will be even more motivated to make the world a better place, for their sakes as well as for those of your human family members and yourself.

Chapter 10

Animal
Wisdom

What
Animals
Can Teach Us

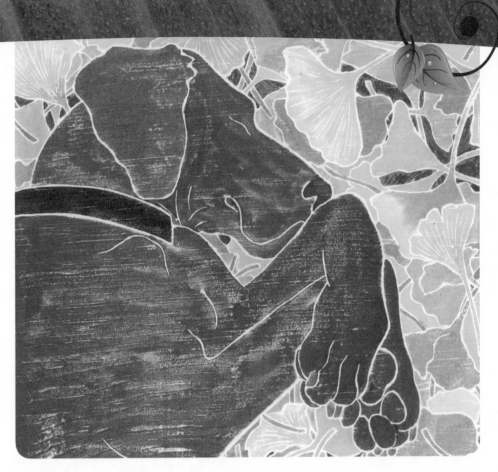

Sometimes, when I'm standing in the kitchen microwaving a cold cup of coffee, Jack and Sally run up to me and start wiggling their butts and wagging their tails and getting all excited, for no apparent reason. A cynic might say that they think me in the kitchen equals a high probability of a treat, and that cynic might be right

(organic chicken liver, anyone?). However, whatever it is they are communicating comes out of them with such a joyful happy wiggle that I can't help smiling and thinking: *dogs just want to have fun.*

Cats are the same way. What drives them to slink over and rub themselves all over your hand until you can't resist returning the caresses? What causes them to

suddenly roll on their backs and bat at invisible playthings dangling in the air? *Cats just want to have fun.*

So do birds, bunnies, horses, goats, chickens, and even mice. Or maybe that's just my rosy perception of things. (I've been accused of that.) Maybe it's more accurate to say that in my view, as a lifelong animal lover and caretaker, animals live in

the present moment and see life just as it is. Anybody who lives with animals and knows them well also knows that they are inspired by feelings and urges, passions and emotions. Our animals are connected to us, and we are connected to them, but they are also directly connected to the natural cycle of life in ways we adult humans can barely remember. Maybe they can remind us.

Instinct

Watch your animal companions for a while, and you are likely to see some expression of instinct. Instinct is a natural behavior that happens without learning. For example, when your hand touches fire, you instinctively pull it away. When you see a child in danger, you instinctively rush to protect her. If something frightens you, you instinctively run away or get ready to fight.

Instinct happens in the so-called primitive brain at the base of the brain, whereas logical thought, decision making, and learning are the realm of the more evolved cerebral cortex. You operate on instinct sometimes, but in humans, our upper brains, our logical brains, are so highly developed that

Green Fact

When baby ducks or geese first see their mother, they instinctually follow her wherever she goes. This is called imprinting. If a baby bird imprints on a human instead, it will follow the human, and when the bird is an adult, it may tend to prefer humans and even try to court them.

they tend to shout louder than our instinctual brains. Sometimes, they shout too loudly and we ignore instincts we shouldn't ignore, like the impulse to get out of a dangerous situation even though our logical brains tell us everything will probably be just fine.

Animals are more in touch with that so-called lower brain, so they tend to act sensibly on instinct more often than we do, even if they don't always puzzle out the subtler cues in a situation. If something frightens them, they flee or fight, whereas we might decide we should rationalize our way out of the situation.

When you spend more time with your companion animals, you will witness more instinct in action. For one thing, many animals—especially dogs—display instincts based on the jobs they traditionally performed for or with humans. Herding breeds naturally tend to herd sheep (or cats or children) without any training. They might nip at heels or push people in one direction or another to get the "flock" under control.

Guardian breeds patrol the perimeter of their property, carefully eyeing the area for any intruders. If they sense danger, they go into alert or even attack mode. Fortunately, in healthy, well-bred dogs, that danger sense is often fairly accurate, and they won't attack someone who isn't a threat. (Poor training and socialization can mess up that instinct, however.)

Terriers have a natural instinct to chase small animals up trees or down into their burrows, hounds will follow a scent trail with virtually no training, and hunting dogs can become obsessed with bird watching, retrieving, or naturally pointing to a bird they see in the yard.

In some ways, humans "created" these instincts in dogs by breeding together those dogs who naturally displayed the traits we wanted to encourage. Whether you think humans should have done this or not, the fact is that humans and dogs have a very long, complex working relationship, and this is the result.

Humans aren't so different from animals. Those humans who bonded with and depended on dogs for survival were probably more likely to survive in certain cultures and environments, which could have prompted a real evolutionary change in our species, from a biped that minded his own business to a biped with a deep soft spot in his heart for dogs.

But can we learn even more about instinct from our companion animals? I think that we can. Notice the way your dog listens when he hears a noise outside or the way your cat peers at a bird outside the window. Watch how their movements change when they feel safe, when they go into guard mode, or when they stalk something in the grass. Then, start listening to your own inner voice. What are your instincts telling you?

Observation

Animals have incredible powers of observation. Humans have a lot of mental chatter going on because we are almost always thinking. Thinking, thinking, thinking. All that thinking makes it difficult to pay attention to what is going on right here, right now, because thinking usually shoots us back into the past or launches us into the future.

Animals live *now*. Maybe they think about the past or the future. We can't be sure. But spend your own time observing them, and you'll see how tuned in they are to the immediate environment. Ears move forward or rise up. Tails twitch. Hair rises at the nape of the neck. Legs crouch. Eyes narrow. Or skin goes soft, eyes close, body rolls over in luxurious sun worship or total immersion in the wonderful feeling of being stroked.

Can we learn from that? For thousands of years, people have tried. Meditation is a great way to practice your own powers of observation or mindfulness. Sit quietly in a comfortable spot where you will be undisturbed for a while, and just observe. What do you see? What do you hear, within the room and outside of it? What do you feel? The air on your skin? Heat or cold? Your clothing? Your hair? What do you smell? Just five or ten minutes of this kind of mindful meditation every day can make a huge difference in how well your brain works, not to mention how observant and sensitive to your environment you can become. Try it. Your cat will definitely approve.

Conservation

Jack and Sally may not always finish everything in their food bowls, but I've never seen them dump anything in the trash. In fact, they are much more likely to pull things *out* of the trash, as if to say, "Hey, why are you throwing this away? We can still *use* this!" They are *so* green.

Animals are naturals at conservation. Going out and buying more stuff is obviously not on their radars, but they know exactly how to use what they have and find new uses for things we thought were trash. They find spaces to sleep, play, and exercise wherever they are. No doghouse? That cozy spot under the desk is just fine. No sunny meadow? The squares of sun on the living room floor will do. Dogs bury bones and hide food so they can come back to them later, and cats are excellent at conserving their energy so they have it when they need it. Is there a lesson in that?

You know there is. What if you had to go for a week, a month, or even a year without buying anything new? Could you figure out how to get what you need from the things you already have? Can you make the most of the food you have so you don't waste it?

Can you learn how to slow down, rest, and bask in the sun a bit, so you have energy when you need it for all the work you have to do? Try living like an animal for a day, and see how it feels. It's fun, it's free, and it's certainly eco-friendly.

Simplicity

Your animals might like watching Animal Planet or the Discovery Channel with you, but do you really think they would complain if you turned off the tube? They like watching TV with you because they are with *you*. To an animal, it's the companionship that matters.

That's not to say animals don't like action. They love to exercise and spend time outside. They enjoy eating and sleeping and grooming themselves. Sometimes they play with whatever is at hand, and sometimes they just sit or lie around doing nothing. Most of them enjoy interacting with other animals and other people, but animals don't need equipment or a rule book or a league to play on a team. They don't need a flickering screen to stay amused, and they certainly don't need to go shopping.

What if your needs were that simple? Maybe they are. It can take some time to get used to simpler pleasures, but it's all a matter of habit. What if you didn't watch television for a week? What if you just ate your meals, got some exercise, groomed

Green Words

"It is the sweet, simple things of life which are the real ones after all."

—Laura Ingalls Wilder,
American author

"To heal our relationship to our bodies is to heal our relationship with the earth."

—Anodea Judith,
American author and therapist

even if we can't do it all at once. And if you get bored or restless? Well, what's your dog or your cat or your bird or your rabbit doing right now? Why not try that?

Animal Zen

This book is nearly at an end, and what I hope you will take away from it, if nothing else, is this: animals are companions worthy of our respect, love, and care, and because they are so close to nature in ways we can only begin to comprehend, they are also the key to our salvation. The earth is facing a crisis, and we have the power to do something about it, but if we just keep spending and wasting and spewing our pollution without any sense of care, stewardship, or respect for the natural world, we may end up in a world of trouble.

yourself, and spent the occasional hour doing absolutely nothing? You probably have a job to do, so do that job and whatever that requires, but when you are done working, do you know how to stop and just be? This is really difficult for some of us, especially because we live in a society that values the overachiever.

But maybe society is on the wrong track. Maybe the animals have a more satisfying take on life. We can probably all do as they do a little bit more in our lives,

Animals understand how to live lightly on the earth, and we can learn from them. We also owe them an immense debt of gratitude. They have served as our loyal and loving companions for many thousands of years, even in the face of abuse, violence, and abandonment.

Our companion animals love on, as part of the natural world, and they remind us that we are part of the natural world, too, and that everything good in us and good in them is what is good about the earth that holds us. We inherited our best traits from our mother the earth. I hope that you will join me in doing everything possible to honor, care for, and protect her.

Green Words

"Tread softly! All the earth is holy ground."

—Christina Rossetti,
English poet

Resources

ONLINE ANIMAL ADOPTION RESOURCES

Alley Cat Rescue: The National Cat Protection Association: www.saveacat.org, acr@saveacat.org, (301) 277-5595. For a list of publications, write to Alley Cat Rescue, Inc., PO Box 585, Mount Ranier, MD 20712. This group works to protect cats locally through rescue and adoption and nationally through a network of cat action teams.

The American Society for the Prevention of Cruelty to Animals: www.aspca.org. To locate a shelter nearby, go to "Ways to Help" column, click "Adopt," then click "Find a Shelter."

Animal Shelter.org: www.animalshelter.org. This Web site has a quick pet search function that allows you to search by zip code according to the kind of animal you seek.

Petfinder: www.petfinder.org. This database contains a comprehensive list of shelters and rescue groups in every state. Search by zip code according to the kind of animal and breed you seek.

Pets911.com: www.pets911.com. This site has links for pet adoption, lost and found pets, shelter and rescue resources, spaying and neutering information, and finding a veterinarian.

Purebred Cat Breed Rescue: www.purebredcatbreedrescue.org. Find a purebred cat through this group.

The Senior Dogs Project: www.srdogs.com. This group specializes in finding homes for adopted senior dogs. Search by state, including Canada.

ANIMAL WELFARE RESOURCES

American Humane Association: www.americanhumane.org, info@americanhumane.org, 63 Inverness Drive East, Englewood, CO 80112, (800) 227-4645. This nonprofit organization is devoted to protecting both children and animals from cruelty, abuse, neglect, and exploitation. This organization works to develop and promote policy and encourage legislation relevant to their cause. They also make education a priority.

American Society for the Prevention of Cruelty to Animals (ASPCA): www.aspca .org. For adoption information, call (212) 876-7700. For the This Web site is full of useful information about animal adoption, behavior, sheltering, anticruelty, disaster readiness, grief counseling, humane law enforcement, animal-related legislation, puppy mills, shelter statistics, spay/neuter information, and veterinary advice, including an excellent resource on poison control.

Best Friends Animal Society: www.bestfriends.org, 5001 Angel Canyon Road, Kanab, UT 84741-5000, (435) 644-2001. My mom hardly ever stops talking about this place, reads their magazine cover to cover the day it arrives, and dreams of going to Utah to visit the Best Friends animal sanctuary. This group does great work and runs an amazing shelter/sanctuary that has served as the model for many other shelters and sanctuaries.

Compassion Over Killing: www.cok.net, info@cok.net, PO Box 9773, Washington, DC 20016. This nonprofit animal advocacy organization works to end animal cruelty and abuse in agri-culture and promotes vegetarianism for a kinder, more compassionate world. On the Web site, you can order a free copy of their *Vegetarian Starter Guide*, get a free e-newsletter, and order pamphlets to hand out. My family ordered a stack of pamphlets called *Eating Sustainably: Fight Global Warming with Your Fork*. My ten-year-old son, Emmett, placed the pamphlets in strategic locations all around his school. To find these publications on the Web site, click on "Marketplace."

Defenders of Wildlife: www.defenders.org, defenders@mail.defenders.org, 1130 17th Street NW, Washington, DC 20036, (800) 385-9712. This group works to protect wolves, polar bears, owls, and other wildlife endangered by global warming, deforestation, pollution, and habitat loss. They are committed to the preservation of biological diversity in the United States.

Farm Sanctuary: www.farmsanctuary.org, info@farmsanctuary.org, PO Box 150, Watkins Glen, NY 14891, (607) 583-2225, rescue hotline (to report potential rescues and cruelty cases) (607) 583-2225, ext. 312. This organization is devoted to caring for animals rescued from slaughter, such as chickens, pigs, goats, cows, and turkeys, by providing homes on their two farms in New York and California. They also work to fight cruel factory farming practices.

House Rabbit Society: www.rabbit.org. This organization is devoted to championing rabbits as individuals with the same rights and intrinsic value as any other companion animal, and to educating the public about their health, welfare, temperament, and relationship to humans. Find your local chapter on their Web site at www.rabbit.org/hrs-info/contacts.html.

Humane Society of the United States: www.hsus.org, 2100 L Street NW, Washington, DC 20037, (202) 452-1100. This large and active organization works to achieve a humane and sustainable world for animals and people. They advocate for public policy in the best interest of animals, fight cruelty, and fund disaster relief and animal sanctuaries as well as wildlife re-habilitation centers and veterinary clinics. They have done a lot to change laws that were cruel to animals and help prosecute those who break those laws. They are deeply involved in such issues as dog fighting, cockfighting, puppy mills, factory farms, unsporting hunting practices, horse slaughter, clubbing baby seals, and the fur trade.

North Shore Animal League: www.nsalamerica.org, 25 Davis Avenue, Port Washington, NY 11050, (516) 883-7575. This is the world's largest no-kill shelter. Members of the league go to great lengths to educate the public about responsible pet ownership. The North Shore Animal League also created Spay USA (www.spayusa.org), a program with the goal of ending euthanasia of adoptable companion animals by encouraging spay/neuter programs all over the United States.

GREEN ORGANIZATIONS

Hemp Industries Association: www.thehia.org, info@thehia.org, 870 Market Street, Suite 1146, San Francisco, CA 94102, (707) 874-3648. A hemp industries trade association actively working to represent the hemp industry, educate the public about the benefits of hemp products, and support socially responsible and eco-friendly business practices.

National Park Service: www.nps.gov. The National Park Service cares for and maintains our country's national parks; we have almost 400 of them. They also help communities by offering grants to help create community parks and recreation facilities, develop trails and greenways, and conserve rivers and streams. They have seven regional offices. Find contact information for your region on the Web site.

Organic Exchange: www.organicexchange.org, 822 Baldridge, O'Donnell, TX 79351, (806) 428-3411. A resource devoted to the production of organic fiber.

Organic Trade Association: www.ota.com, PO Box 547, Greenfield, MA 01302, (413) 774-7511. Find out all about the organic industry from this proactive organization.

Sustainable Cotton Project: www.sustainablecotton.org, PO Box 363, Davis, CA 95617, (530) 756-8518, ext. 34. The Sustainable Cotton Project is a California-based organization working to help California cotton growers reduce pesticide use. Check out their "Fiber Footprint Calculator."

U.S. Fish and Wildlife Services: www.fws.gov. The U.S. Fish and Wildlife Service's mission is "to conserve, protect, and enhance fish, wildlife, and plants and their habitats for the continuing benefit of the American people." They have offices in all fifty states. Find contact information for your state on the Web site.

Vegetarian Resource Group: www.vrg.org, vrg@vrg.org, PO Box 1463, Dept. IN, Baltimore, MD 21203, (410) 366-VEGE. This nonprofit group is "dedicated to educating the public on vegetarianism and the interrelated issues of health, nutrition, ecology, ethics, and world hunger." They publish the *Vegetarian Journal* as well as many other books, pamphlets, and article reprints.

Vote Hemp: www.votehemp.com, hempinfo@votehemp.com, PO Box 1571, Brattleboro, VT 05302, (202) 318-8999. A national nonprofit organization working to change the law that bans hemp farming in the United States.

HEALTH AND HOLISTIC CARE RESOURCES

Academy of Veterinary Homeopathy: www.theavh.org, PO Box 9280, Wilmington, DE 19809, (866) 652-1590. Find a homeopathic veterinarian, or learn more about homeopathy.

American Academy of Veterinary Acupuncture: www.aava.org, PO Box 1058, Glastonbury, CT 06033, (860) 632-9911. Find a veterinary acupuncturist near you using this Web site.

American Holistic Veterinary Medical Association: www.ahvma.org, office@ahvma .org, 2218 Old Emmorton Road, Bel Air, MD 21015, (410) 569-0795. Find a holistic veterinarian through this site, or read up on what holistic medicine is.

American Veterinary Chiropractic Association: www.animalchiropractic.org, 442154 E. 140 Road, Bluejacket, OK 74333, (918) 784-2231. Find a veterinary chiropractor here.

Association of Avian Veterinarians: www.aav.org. Through this organization, find a veterinarian who specializes in birds.

Flower Essence Society: www.flowersociety.org, mail@flowersociety.org, PO Box 459, Nevada City, CA 95959, (800) 736-9222. Find out all about flower essences on this informative page, or contact them for more information about how to use flower essences.

International Association of Animal Massage and Bodywork: www.iaamb.org, info@ iaamb.org, (800) 903-9350. Find an animal bodyworker here.

National Animal Supplement Council: www.nasc.cc, PO Box 2568, Valley Center, CA 92082, (760) 751-3360. This trade organization for animal supplement manufacturers requires all members to practice strict quality-control standards.

GREEN GROOMING PRODUCTS

Canine Earth: www.canineearth.com, (866) 832-2752. This company makes USDA-certified organic grooming products. All ingredients are made in the United States, petrochemical free, and hypoallergenic, with no sulfates, parabens, artificial colors, or fragrances.

Dr. Shawn's Pet Organics: www.drshawnspetorganics.com, animalshealing22@aol.com, PO Box 545, Pound Ridge, NY 10576, (877) 929-1515. A holistic vet, Dr. Messonnier wrote *The Natural Bible for Dogs and Cats* and many other books about the health of animal companions. He also founded of Paws & Claws Animal Hospital in Plano, Texas. He has developed his own line of USDA-certified organic pet shampoos made without any petroleum products, sulfates, dyes, perfumes, or anything synthetic. They are made in the United States in bottles without BPA, and all three formulas have ingredients that heal skin, repel insects, and are antifungal, antibacterial, and anti-inflammatory.

Earthbath Totally Natural Pet Care: www.earthbath.com, info@earthbath.com, PO Box 411050, San Francisco, CA 94141, (415) 355-1166. This company makes all natural, biodegradable pet grooming and care products for dogs and cats. They are phosphate free and hypoallergenic, and contain natural botanicals. They are also cruelty free.

Juno's Garden: www.paldog.com, pals@paldog.com, (888) 738-8390. This California-based company makes organic grooming products for dogs and cats made with organic herbs, human-grade ingredients, and no synthetic ingredients like SLS, DEA, or parabens. All formulas are biodegradable and made in the United States. They make shampoo and bath soap, conditioner, freshening spray, ear wash, and hand cream for people (because holiding that dog leash can chafe!).

NuHemp: www.nuhemp.com, info@nuhemp.com, 5551 Highway 6 North, Guelph, ON, Canada, (519) 836-8443. This company makes products from sustainable, renewable hemp, including nutritional supplements, treats, and small animal bedding, as well as eco-friendly grooming products for skin and coat. There are great formulas for shampooing, detangling, odor control, and itch relief. All formulas are made with botanical ingredients, many certified organic.

Spot Organics: www.spotorganics.com, contact@spotorganics.com, 774 Shady Drive E, Pittsburgh, PA 15228, (412) 901-5879. This company bases its products on aromatherapy and 100 percent natural ingredients. It makes sweet-smelling organic shampoos for dogs for banishing fleas, improving coat quality, and getting rid of itchy skin. It also makes an all-natural flea spray, a calming spray, a skin spray, a spray for bedding, a breath spray, ear-cleaning products, and some essential oil blends. Plus, it uses recyclable bottles and the shampoo is biodegradable.

Vermont Soap Organics: www.vermontsoap.com, info@vermontsoap.com, 616 Exchange Street, Middlebury, VT 05753, (866) 762-7482. This company, makes certified organic pet shampoo with organic coconut, olive, and jojoba oils, organic aloe vera, and other natural and organic essential oils. Preserved with natural rosemary extract, the shampoo is mild, hypoallergenic, and free of petroleum and animal by-products. It meets USDA organic food standards. There is also a horse shampoo, soap for people, a yoga mat wash, and a fruit and veggie wash.

GREEN ODOR/STAIN CONTROL PRODUCTS

Earth Friendly Products: www.ecos.com. This company makes products for the whole house that contain no animal ingredients and are never tested on animals. Its cleaners are totally plant based and all paper used is recycled. Animal-relevant products include an excellent stain and odor remover, a laundry detergent for your pet's clothes and bedding, a spray for skin and coat that removes body odor and can even reduce allergic reactions in people sensitive to pet dander, pet wipes for paws (with no irritating-skin oils), a natural chew deterrent spray, a skunk odor remover, a kitty litter treatment formula, and a bird-enclosure cleaner.

Fresh Wave: www.fresh-wave.com. This company's sprays, gels, vacuum pearls, candles, and cleaning fluids work so well, it's hard to believe. These products are made by a company with a long history of odor control in industrial environments, so they have had to invent ways to deal with odor far beyond anything your dog or cat could cough up.

Petrotech: www.sea-yu.com, (877) 854-6624. This San Francisco-based company makes a nitrogen-propelled odor eliminator that won't damage the ozone and is nontoxic and completely biodegradable. According to the company, this product is totally ecologically friendly. Petrotech is rigorous about its manufacturing process and also about using environmentally friendly packaging. Its brochures are printed on 100 percent recycled paper using 100 percent certified renewable energy, and meet the Forest Stewardship Council's standards for responsible forest management, as well as being Smartwood certified, a Rainforest Alliance program.

ECO-CONSCIOUS PET FOOD, TREAT, AND SUPPLEMENT COMPANIES

Bite O' Blue Wild Blueberry Dog Treats: www.biteoblue.com, (207) 843-6484. This company makes crunchy dog biscuits loaded with antioxidant-rich organic Maine wild lowbush blueberries and other human-grade ingredients, which the company handcrafts on its Peaked Mountain Farm in Dedham, Maine. The farm has been in the family since 1868. Best of all, the treats are baked via wind power from the farm's wind turbine, for a truly eco-friendly treat, packed in recyclable and biodegradable packaging. On its Web site, the company says, "We believe being 'green' is everybody's job; even the dog's."

Eagle Pack Pet Foods: www.eaglepack.com, (574) 259-7834. These foods contain hypoallergenic ingredients like duck meal, organic quinoa, and fruits and vegetables. They base their formulas on meat meal from human food sources and only use whole grains. They are balanced, excellent foods, manufactured in Mishawaka, Indiana.

Halo, Purely for Pets: www.halopurelyforpets.com, (800) 426-4256. This company, based in Palm Harbor, Florida, got started when president Andi Brown started feeding her own pets her homemade Spot's Stew, then decided to produce it for others. She also has a great book that tells you how to make your own pet food: *The Whole Pet Diet*, by Andi Brown (Celestial Arts, 2006).

Honest Kitchen: www.thehonestkitchen.com. The Honest Kitchen makes dehydrated raw dog food and treats from 100 percent human-grade ingredients in a human food plant in California.

The products contain no chemical preservatives, by-products, salt, sugar, or artificial colors or flavors, and no beet pulp, rice, wheat, corn, or soy (common dog food fillers). This is a company with a lot of integrity and a passion for dogs. People taste-test every batch, and they package all products with a combination of USA-made 100 percent recycled, biodegradable paper and partially postconsumer recycled plastic.

In Clover: www.inclover.com, (303) 581-9619. This company, located in Boulder, Colorado, is a member of the National Animal Supplement Council, which requires rigorous quality control standards. They make supplements that support joints, digestion, and dental health. They are a small, friendly, ethical company with great products.

Lazy Dog Cookie Company, Inc.: www.lazydogcookies.com, 27 Kent Street, Suite 105A, Ballston Spa, NY 12026, (518) 309-3732. This company hand makes beautiful frosted and decorated soft-baked dog cookies in its bakery. In 2007, it switched over to 100 percent organic human-grade ingredients sourced entirely in the United States, containing no wheat, corn, or soy. All the toppings, which look like sugar and candy, are actually 100 percent real freeze-dried fruits, nuts, and vegetables so the treats make great guilt-free gifts for fellow animal and earth lovers. Husband and wife team Keith and Amy Augustine also recently joined the Organic Trade Association and are now in the process of printing all new packaging with soy ink on 35 percent postconsumer recycled paperboard.

Merrick Pet Care, Inc.: www.merrickpetcare.com and www.beforegrain.com, (800) 664-7387. This family company in Amarillo, Texas, keeps their food manufacturing processes simple with basic ingredients everyone recognizes. One of the company's new lines, B.G. (Before Grain), includes multiple high-quality meat sources for nutritional variety and other interesting ingredients such as açai berries, sustainably produced in the Amazon rainforest and contain high levels of healthful antioxidants. The dry foods contain essential fatty acids and beneficial vegetables and herbs, and the company also makes 100 percent meat canned food. It is not a complete diet but it is a convenient way to supplement kibble. My dogs particularly like the tripe.

Natura Pet Products: www.naturapet.com. This company, based in Santa Clara, California, makes several excellent brands of food for animal companions, including Karma (organic), Innova, Evo, California Natural, HealthWise, and a treat line called Mother Nature. This is a larger company than many of the companies I like, but in my dealings with the people there, I have found them to be sincerely committed to what is best for animals, with exceptionally high standards for the company's foods and manufacturing processes.

Newman's Own Organics: www.newmansownorganics.com. This line of food has the quality you would expect from Newman's Own. It is USDA-certified organic, using free-range organic protein sources such as human-grade chicken and free-range beef from Uruguay. Uruguay is recognized as one of the cleanest countries in the world, with 270 organic beef farms certified free of E. coli and bovine spongiform encephalopathy ("mad cow disease"). The energy required to transport beef from Uruguay is probably well worth it because of the quality of this grass-fed and humanely treated beef. Plus, Newman's Own donates all profits from the sale of their organic foods to charitable organizations. Paul Newman's daughter Nell has designated all profits from Newman's Own pet foods to go to organizations that support the well-being of animals.

Old Mother Hubbard: www.oldmotherhubbard.com, (800) 225-0904. This company makes dog biscuits, treats, and canned dog food using only 100 percent whole-food, human-grade ingredients.

Oxbow Animal Health: www.oxbowanimalhealth.com, (800) 249-0366. For all of you small-animal lovers out there, this Nebraska company makes organic pellets for guinea pigs and rabbits, organic meadow hay, organic barley biscuits, and all-natural pelleted wheat straw litter. For small animals, the company also makes little tunnels, loungers, and "bungalows" that are made out of chemical-free Timothy hay with no wires or threads. The products are USDA organic certified.

PetGuard: www.petguard.com, petcare@petguard.com or customerservice@petguard .com. This Florida company is probably best known for its vegetarian dog foods. It also makes organic dry and canned food, and some of its foods and treats are vegan, containing no animal products of any kind. Needless to say, these foods have no by-products or artificial ingredients. In addition, PetGuard makes a good organic cat food (not vegetarian) as well as cat treats with organic catnip and other ingredients for good dental health.

Primal: www.primalpetfoods.com, sales@primalpetfoods.com, (866) 566-4652. This California company makes 100 percent human-grade raw food for both dogs and cats. Their foods are made with meat, poultry, and game free of antibiotics, hormones, or steroids from U.S.-based ranches practicing sustainable agriculture.

So Bright: www.sobrightllc.com, (888) 894-1973. This Evergreen, Colorado company's food and treats are USDA-certified organic.

Sojourner Farms: www.sojos.com, (888) 867-6567. This Minneapolis-based company makes several different mixes, which are meant to be combined with fresh raw or cooked meat for a complete diet. A cool product and a great company, in my experience.

Stella & Chewy's: www.stellaandchewys.com, (888) 477-8977. This great company makes frozen and freeze-dried raw dog and cat food with no preservatives, chemicals, hormones, antibiotics, sugar, or salt. The food is designed to mimic the exact proportion of meat, bone, and organic fruits and vegetables an animal would eat in the wild. FDA-inspected, the plants treats all the food with water pressure to eliminate pathogens. Each batch is tested for *Salmonella* and *E. coli* in an independent laboratory, and the company posts all the results on its Web site.

Wellness: www.wellnesspetfood.com, (800) 225-0904. This company, based in Tewksbury, Massachusetts, makes dry and canned foods, including grain-free and allergy-free formulas. It also makes supplements for joint support and healthy skin and coat, as well as 100 percent human-grade dog biscuits and gourmet treats under the Old Mother Hubbard label.

Wild Kitty: www.wildkittycatfood.com, (207) 985-6134. This company makes 100 percent all-natural raw cat food that is organically sterilized for safety. It also produces "Make Your Own Cat Food" kits, so people can buy their own meat and just add the kit ingredients for a complete diet.

GREEN BEDS, TOYS, LEASHES, AND MORE PRODUCTS

Big Shrimpy: www.bigshrimpy.com, (206) 297-7918. This Montana-based company is deeply committed to sustainable living. Big Shrimpy produces comfortable, cushy beds for dogs and cats; the beds are manufactured using salvaged waste materials from other industries. The company's beds are so high quality that your animals will probably be able to use them for their entire lives, thus reducing waste. You can remove the stuffing and machine wash the beds easily, too. In 2006, 96 percent of Big Shrimpy's product sales revenue came from products using at least 50 percent recycled material. The company recycled 75,200 pounds of fleece scraps salvaged from clothing manufactures in North America to use in its pet beds that year.

Good Dog Company: www.thegooddogcompany.com, (866) 433-6426. The company makes earth-friendly collars, harnesses, leashes, and toys out of hemp and organic cotton. Based in Golden, Colorado, the Good Dog Company not only uses sustainable materials in its manufacturing but also makes all its products with local workers, emphasizing American craftsmanship. The company recycles manufacturing waste and donates part of the profits to environmental and social causes at the local and national level.

Itzadog: www.itzadog.com, (800) 961-2364. Itzadog manufactures collars and leashes that are made from retired, recycled advertising billboards. The Itzadog collars are durable and weatherproof, and each one of them is totally unique because the billboards that they come from are all different.

Planet Dog: www.planetdog.com, customerservice@planetdog.com, (800) 381-1516. This is an active, socially responsible company with great products and a strong commitment to philanthropy. It makes toys, collars, leashes, treats, beds, puppy supplies, supplements, travel supplies, grooming supplies, gifts, and apparel, and it is always coming out with interesting and innovative new products. Two percent of every purchase goes into the Planet Dog Foundation, which promotes and celebrates service dogs, such as therapy dogs, assistance dogs, search and rescue dogs, police dogs, and bomb-sniffing dogs. Planet Dog awards grants to fund working dog programs as well as environmental, animal welfare, and educational programs. The company's mantra is: *Think globally, act doggedly.*

Purrfectplay: www.purrfectplay.com, (219) 926-7604. The company handcrafts natural organic dye-free toys and other products for cats and dogs, such as catnip toys, wool balls, plush organic fabric bones, hemp rope chew toys, dye-free wool tug toys, hemp dog bandanas, cotton fleece beds and sleep pouches, dye-free hemp collars, and bags of certified organic catnip. It also crafts collar charms made of fair-trade Thai mountain silver with polished midwestern river stones, felted sweater leash and treat pouches, hemp washcloths, stainless steel water canteens, and USDA-certified organic, human-grade dog treats. This little Indiana company is passionately committed to making the environment and products safe and nontoxic for our pets. Contact the company, and sign up for the free e-newsletter so you can stay on top of the latest environmental issues affecting pets.

RocknRollK9: www.rocknrollk9.com, (781) 576-9936. This company makes cool T-shirts, "for the four-legged rock star." You can get a T-shirt to match your dog's! Owner Mark Baizen took inspiration from old sixties rock posters, adapted them to have a dog theme, and put them on his T-shirts. Best of all, the shirts are 100 percent certified organic baby rib cotton, and not just in order to make the shirts soft. The Massachusetts-based company says that when you purchase one of its T-shirts, you are: "Helping to conserve biodiversity, reduce global warming, naturally enrich the soil, create healthier working conditions for agricultural workers, keep tons of chemicals out of the environment, minimize damage to ecosystems, and support efficient farming practices."

Silly Kitty: www.sillykitty.ca, (866) 557-5915. This Canadian company manufacturers hemp products such as toys and leashes. If you are afraid that your pet will eat his toys, try these. Hemp is completely digestible. Cats love the signature Silly Kitty toy, and I like the hemp corduroy leashes.

Simply Fido: www.simplyfido.com, (718) 389-8233. This company makes beautiful pet toys out of untreated organic cotton hand-dyed in soy water, so the toys are completely chemical free, because pets put toys in their mouths. There are cotton plush toys, knitted cotton toys, and natural hemp toys, all with squeakers, and cotton blankets for puppies. Simply Fido uses a specialized natural filtering system to purify its waste water from the coloring process, before releasing the water back into the environment, to reduce any negative impact. Although the Brooklyn-based company's manufacturing facility is in Shanghai, the company says, "By following the highest international labor standards, our employees are treated with respect. We make sure they are happy, healthy, and compensated fairly for all their hard work. Being environmentally responsible and treating workers the right way go hand in hand."

Wagging Green: www.wagginggreen.com, (321) 610-4426. Wagging Green makes bamboo fiber dog collars, harnesses, leashes, dog tags, and dog T-shirts. The bamboo is natural, undyed, 100 percent organic. Bamboo is biodegradable, contains no pesticides or fertilizers, and is naturally breathable and thermal regulating. The Wagging Green products are all hand sewn in North America. The company also uses its product packaging to educate consumers about solar power, reducing greenhouse gas emissions, cleaning up the oceans, saving endangered species, supporting alternative energy sources, and the eco-friendly nature of bamboo fiber. Wagging Green gives back 5 percent of its profits to green causes. The company's motto is: *Saving the earth one dog at a time.*

West Paw Design: www.westpawdesign.com, (800) 443-5567. This company, based, which is based in Montana, makes eco-friendly dog and cat beds, pillows, mats, plush toys, tug toys, squeak toys, feather toys, catnip toys, and fun holiday toys. The products are constructed from recycled materials.

BIODEGRADABLE POOP BAGS, CAT PAN LINERS, AND LITTER

BioBags: www.biobagusa.com. This company was the first to popularize the biodegradable "plastic" poop bags.

Feline Pine: www.naturesearth.com. This is the litter made from recycled wood dust and remnants, which the company reclaims from lumberyards. It forms the pine dust into pellets, but the litter itself is dust free, completely natural, and the Feline Pine Scoop variety even clumps.

Flush Doggy: www.flushdoggy.com. These bags are actually flushable and 100 percent biodegradable so you don't have to dump the poop out of the bag and into the toilet. The company also donates 10 percent of its profits to the ASPCA to help pets.

NuHemp: www.nuhemp.com, info@nuhemp.com, 5551 Highway 6 North, Guelph, ON, Canada, (519) 836-8443. This company makes great products out of sustainable, renewable hemp, grown legally in Canada. One of its great products is safe, clean, dust-free, antimicrobial, absorbent bedding material for rabbits, small animals, birds, and horses. It is called BIO-Nesting, and it is made out of the inner core and outer fibers of the hemp plant.

PlanetWise Products: www.planetwiseproducts.com. This company makes all-natural pine pellet litter in regular and clumping formulas for cats, as well as pine pellet bedding for horse stalls, small animal enclosures, and bird enclosures. Normally, you shouldn't use pine shavings for small animals because they can cause health problems, but the *Cozy 'n Fresh* product is sterile and has all the aromatic hydrocarbons and irritating oils removed, so it's perfectly safe.

Poop Bags: www.poopbags.com. These bags biodegrade at about the same rate as an apple, according to the company and meet ASTM D6400 specifications for biodegradability, which some states require of any product claiming to be biodegradable. The bags are made from renewable products like corn. The company also makes biodegradable cat pan liners.

Swheat Scoop: www.swheatscoop.com, (800) 794-3287. Produced via strip mining, clay litters never decompose. This natural wheat litter is renewable, biodegradable, and great at nixing litter box odor. Produced from naturally processed secondary wheat, it not only is an environmentally friendly product but also contains no dust and is safe for cats and kittens, even if ingested.

World's Best Cat Litter: www.worldsbestcatlitter.com. This brand is flushable and made from whole-kernel corn, which has a microporous structure the company says absorbs odor without any added chemicals or perfumes. It is dust free and won't harm cats if they ingest some of it.

Yesterday's News: www.yesterdaysnews.com. This litter is made from recycled newspapers, and the company says its manufacturing process neutralizes ink residue so the product is nontoxic. This litter is not flushable. Fill the litter box with two or three inches. The litter absorbs from the bottom, so change it often and keep an eye on what is going on at the bottom level.

GREEN PRODUCTS FOR YOUR HOME, GARAGE, AND GARDEN

SafeLawns.org: www.safelawns.org, info@safelawns.org., Maine office (207) 688-8882, Washington, DC office (202) 544-5430. This nonprofit group is dedicated to organic lawn care.

Safe Paw: www.safepaw.com, (800) 783-7841. This is a salt-free, environmentally friendly, nontoxic deicing product.

Sierra Antifreeze/Coolant: www.sierraantifreeze.com, (800) 323-5440. Sierra is the industry leader in safer, more environmentally friendly propylene glycol-based antifreeze.

GREEN BLOGS, WEB SITES, AND OTHER ONLINE SOURCES

City Farmer: www.cityfarmer.org. This interesting Web site has a video that shows you exactly how to install your own pet waste septic system.

Cool Vegan.com: www.coolvegan.com. This Web site has a huge list of links related to living the vegan and vegetarian lifestyle.

Green is the New Red: www.greenisthenewred.com. This blog tracks instances of activists for environmental, animal, antiwar, or other causes being targeted as so-called terrorists. The focus is on "how fear of 'terrorism' is being exploited to push a political and corporate agenda." Specifically, it focuses on "how animal rights and environmental advocates are being branded 'eco-terrorists' in what many are calling the Green Scare." It also has a link to the National Lawyers Guide "Green Scare Hotline," for any activist who has experienced harassment: (888) NLG-ECOL.

Grinning Planet: www.grinningplanet.com. This fun Web site takes a humorous and entertaining but also serious approach to environmental issues.

Living Green Below Your Means: www.newdream.org/lgbym. Get hints and inspiration to help you live the eco-friendly life without busting your budget.

New American Dream: www.newdream.org. It issues challenges to help us live greener.

Organic Gardening Magazines: www.organicgardening.com. This is the popular magazine's online presence.

Pets for the Environment: www.petsfortheenvironment.org. This fun blog is "written" by a dog named Eddie, and will keep you up to date on environmental issues directly related to pets, like pet food testing, toxins in toys, and "green" cat litter.

Pets Welcome: www.petswelcome.com. This site lists over 1,800 pet-friendly hotels and features travel tips.

Vegetarian Resource Group: www.vrg.org, vrg@vrg.org, PO Box 1463, Dept. IN, Baltimore, MD 21203, (410) 366-VEGE. This nonprofit group is "dedicated to educating the public on veg-etarianism and the interrelated issues of health, nutrition, ecology, ethics, and world hunger." The group publishes the *Vegetarian Journal* as well as books, pamphlets, and article reprints.

Vegetarian Restaurants: www.vegetarian-restaurants.net. Enter your state and locate some vegetarian-friendly restaurants near you.

VegFamily: www.vegfamily.com. This online magazine supports people who are raising vegan children.

VegWeb: www.vegweb.com. If you are looking for some great vegetarian recipes, you should check out this Web site.

Vote Smart: www.votesmart.org. To discover what the politicians who are running your state and the country really think based on how they have voted and what public statements they have made, go to this Web site. Project Vote Smart is a self-proclaimed "factual, non-biased" source of political information that calls itself "The Voter's Self-Defense System." You can search by the last names of the politicians or by your zip code to find out a lot of really interesting information about your elected officials.

HELPFUL BOOKS AND MAGAZINES ABOUT ANIMALS

Adopting a Pet for Dummies, by Eve Adamson, Wiley, 2005.

Cat Fancy, Dog Fancy, Hobby Farms, and many other magazines published by BowTie Inc. that are devoted to our animal companions: www.animalchannel.com.

Chowhound: Dog Treat Baking Book, by Eve Adamson, Sterling, 2009.

Dr. Pitcairn's New Complete Guide to Natural Health for Dogs and Cats, by Richard H. Pitcairn and Susan Hubble Pitcairn, Rodale Books, 2005.

Eco Dog, by Corbett Marshall and Jim Deskevich, Chronicle Books, 2008.

The Goldsteins' Wellness & Longevity Program Natural Care for Dogs and Cats, by Robert S. Goldstein, VMD, and Susan J. Goldstein, TFH, 2005.

Herbs for Pets, by Gregory L. Tilford and Mary L. Wulff, 2nd ed., BowTie Press, 2009.

The Hidden Life of Dogs, by Elizabeth Marshall Thomas, Pocket Books, 1993.

The Nature of Animal Healing: The Definitive Holistic Medicine Guide to Caring for Your Dog and Cat, by Martin Goldstein, DVM, Ballantine Books, 2000.

Natural Health Bible for Dogs and Cats, by Dr. Shawn Messonnier, Three Rivers Press, 2000.

The New Natural Cat: A Complete Guide for Finicky Owners, newly revised and expanded, by Anitra Frazier with Norma Eckroate, Plume, 1990.

Real Food for Dogs: 50 Vet-Approved Recipes to Please the Canine Gastronome, by Arden Moore, Storey Publishing, 2001.

The Ultimate Dog Treat Cookbook: Homemade Goodies for Man's Best Friend, by Liz Palika, Howell Book House, 2005.

Whole Dog Journal: A Monthly Guide to Natural Dog Care and Training, www.whole-dog-journal.com.

The Whole Pet Diet: Eight Weeks to Great Health for Dogs and Cats, by Andi Brown, Celestial Arts, 2006.

HELPFUL GENERAL (NOT ANIMAL-RELATED) BOOKS ABOUT GREEN LIVING

Easy Green Living, by Renée Loux, Rodale, 2008.

The Green Book, by Elizabeth Rogers and Thomas M. Kostigen, Three Rivers Press, 2007.

Living Green: A Practical Guide to Simple Sustainability, by Greg Horn, Freedom Press, 2006.

Skinny Bitch, by Rory Freedman and Kim Barnouin, Running Press, 2005.

The Vegan Sourcebook, by Joanne Stepaniak, 2nd ed., McGraw Hill, 2000.

Vegan with a Vengeance, by Isa Chandra Moskowitz, Da Capo Press, 2005.

Veganomicon, by Isa Chandra Moskowitz, Da Capo Press, 2007.

Illustrations

The images in *Pets Gone Green* represent artist Willy Reddick's personal and organic print-making capturing peaceful moments with people's well-loved pets. The method of color printmaking known as the Provincetown Print (also called white-line woodblock), developed in Provincetown, Massachusetts, in 1916, is a color woodcut in which the line drawing is cut into a single block. Gouache (a type of paint consisting of pigment suspended in water) is applied with a brush, one area at a time; the attached paper is laid down and rubbed with a wooden spoon to print that area only, and so on. The result is a unique print with a painterly quality in which the line drawing remains strong and integral to the finished piece. Willy had been practicing this art since the mid-1990s.

Index

About the author

Eve Adamson is an award-winning freelance writer, a *New York Times* best-selling author, and the author or coauthor of more than fifty books, including many books about companion animals, holistic health, and food. She is a contributing editor and columnist for *Dog Fancy* magazine, writes the "Good Grooming" column for the American Kennel Club's *Family Dog* magazine, and writes the Holistic Marketplace column for *Pet Product News International*.

Eve is a member of the board of directors of the Dog Writers Association of America and a member of the Cat Writers Association, Inc. She has a master of fine arts degree in creative writing from the University of Florida. She lives in Iowa City with her partner, two sons, two dogs, two birds, and assorted oversize goldfish. Find out more about Eve on her Web site at www.eveadamson.com.

ABOUT THE illustrator

Willy Reddick was born in Boston and grew up in an encouraging family of professional artists. She studied at the Massachusetts College of Art and has been working professionally as a painter and white-line woodblock printmaker for more than twenty years.

She is well known for her meditative images of sleeping dogs and cats on busy, vibrant patterns and regularly exhibits in galleries and museums around New England. Her work is also in the collection of the New Bedford Whaling Museum as well as in countless private collections.

In addition to producing woodcuts, she designs and manufactures her own line of Willy Wires jewelry, is a freelance designer, who, among other things, hand paints prototypes for the toy industry, and is a founding partner of Åarhus Gallery (www .aarhusgallery.com) in Belfast, Maine, where she lives with her husband, Wesley, a sculptor, and three cats. For more on Willy and her work, visit her Web site at www .willyreddick.com.